"Of all the valuable information to be found in this work, as a therapist, I particularly recommend the chapter on 'What We Want Therapists and Guidance Counselors to Know.' If you have NLD or know someone who is seeking support from a therapist, you will find it worthwhile to follow Murphy's suggestions and caveats. It is essential that the therapist to whom you turn be exceptionally knowledgeable about the disorder and be competent to provide the guidance that will help you overcome the distresses this disorder may cause you."

—*Joseph Palombo, Director, The Joseph Palombo Center*
for Neuroscience and Psychoanalytic Social Work

"This book will be an eye-opener for teachers, parents, and other interested readers. No doubt many will realize, 'Ahhh, now I understand…' and, hopefully, that understanding will contribute to the success of children and adults with NLD. It's also a valuable resource for young people with NLD: real-life voices, experiences, and common sense. As the parent of an adult child with disabilities, I've learned that the true experts in the field are people with disabilities; Mr. Murphy's book ably demonstrates that fact. Bravo!"

—*Kathie Snow, Author of* Disability is Natural: Revolutionary
Common Sense for Raising Successful Children
with Disabilities *(www.disablityisnatural.com)*

D1293942

NLD from the INSIDE OUT

of related interest

Understanding Nonverbal Learning Disabilities
A Common-Sense Guide for Parents and Professionals
Maggie Mamen
ISBN 978 1 84310 593 0
eISBN 978 1 84642 674 2
JKP Essentials

Helping Children with Nonverbal Learning Disabilities to Flourish
A Guide for Parents and Professionals
Marilyn Martin
ISBN 978 1 84310 858 0
eISBN 978 1 84642 619 3

Understanding Motor Skills in Children with Dyspraxia, ADHD, Autism, and Other Learning Disabilities
A Guide to Improving Coordination
Lisa A. Kurtz
ISBN 978 1 84310 865 8
eISBN 978 1 84642 672 8
JKP Essentials

Making Sense of Children's Thinking and Behavior
A Step-by-Step Tool for Understanding Children with NLD, Asperger's, HFA, PDD-NOS, and other Neurological Differences
Leslie Holzhauser-Peters and Leslie True
ISBN 978 1 84310 888 7
eISBN 978 1 84642 816 6

Raising NLD Superstars
What Families with Nonverbal Learning Disabilities Need to Know about Nurturing Confident, Competent Kids
Marcia Brown Rubinstien
Foreword by Pamela Tanguay
ISBN 978 1 84310 770 5

Employment for Individuals with Asperger Syndrome or Non-Verbal Learning Disability
Stories and Strategies
Yvona Fast
ISBN 978 1 84310 766 8
eISBN 978 1 84642 015 3

NLD from the
INSIDE OUT

Talking to Parents, Teachers, and Teens about
Growing Up with Nonverbal Learning Disabilities

Third Edition

MICHAEL BRIAN MURPHY

Jessica Kingsley *Publishers*
London and Philadelphia

First published in 2016
by Jessica Kingsley Publishers
73 Collier Street
London N1 9BE, UK
and
400 Market Street, Suite 400
Philadelphia, PA 19106, USA

www.jkp.com

Library of Congress Cataloging in Publication Data
Names: Murphy, Michael Brian, 1981-
Title: NLD from the inside out : talking to parents, teachers, and teens about
growing up with nonverbal learning disabilities / Michael Brian Murphy.
Other titles: Nonverbal learning disabilities from the inside out
Description: Third edition. | London ; Philadelphia : Jessica Kingsley
Publishers, 2016. | Includes bibliographical references and index.
Identifiers: LCCN 2016001771 | ISBN 9781849057141 (alk. paper)
Subjects: LCSH: Nonverbal learning disabilities. | Learning disabilities.
Classification: LCC RJ506.L4 M87 2016 | DDC 618.92/85889--dc23 LC record
available at http://lccn.loc.gov/2016001771

British Library Cataloguing in Publication Data
A CIP catalogue record for this book is available from the British Library

ISBN 978 1 84905 714 1
eISBN 978 1 78450 213 3

Printed and bound in the United States

To Dan Turnbull

Contents

Disclaimer

This book does not constitute legal, professional, or medical advice. Readers should exercise judgment in researching information and making decisions about their respective situations.

Acknowledgments

My grateful thanks to the following people.

- The interview subjects and survey respondents, who generously shared their stories.

- The parents, teachers, and NLDers who emailed me with their questions and comments, so that this book could take the shape that it did.

- All of the professionals, authors, and researchers whose work came before mine.

- My mother, Gail Shapiro, for everything, including being a great editor, plus for granting permission to include in Part IV some of the charts and organizational tools she created as she was raising me.

- Special shout-outs to those who gave me advice, encouragement, and/or helped contribute to this project:

  - my family, especially my grandparents, Arline and Harold Shapiro, and my stepfather, Gilbert Wolin; Professors David Stevens, James Laird, and Michael Bamberg at Clark University; Katharine Berlin, Dr. A. Rae Simpson, Catherine Gronewold, Dr. Sandy Miller-Jacobs, Dr. Scott Sokol, Dr. Nick Dubin, Gayle Alexander, and Dan Turnbull.

- All of my teachers, Special Education teachers, and disability services staff members throughout the years, as well as my various doctors, therapists, and diagnosticians, with a special mention to:

  - Professor Everett Fox, Professor Diane Harper, Rabbi Lawrence Kushner, Daniel Pellegrini, Dr. Frank Smith, Marcia Tangerini, and Susie Rodenstein.

- Angela and Richard Hoy and the BookLocker staff for giving me a shot at success by publishing the first two editions of this book.

- Suzanne Connelly, Emma Holak, Rachel Menzies, and the Jessica Kingsley Publishers staff for helping me out so much with this edition.

- Cliff Kolovson and Ray Ringston, for making the website look sweet.

- And finally, to every one of you who took the time to read this book and to learn more about NLD.

Preface to the Third Edition

Dear Reader,

Thank you for purchasing the third edition of *NLD from the Inside Out*. When I first undertook the writing of the first edition, I did so for a few key reasons. First and foremost, I felt as though no one understood me and I needed to tell "the world" (translation: my friends, family, and teachers) my story, just to get it off my chest. But then, the more I learned about my condition, the more I realized that I was not alone. And while on one level, that was a relief for me, it also meant that if the estimated 1 percent of the population who have Nonverbal Learning Disabilities (NLD) figure is accurate, then more than 3 million people in the U.S. alone have NLD—whether diagnosed or not.

Those more than 3 million people are out there, like me, living in limbo, too "normal" to be "disabled;" too "disabled" to be "normal." And more than 3 million people are living their lives with family members, teachers, co-workers, and friends who are flummoxed by what to make of them and by what NLD actually is, and/or who are in denial that having NLD is a legitimate problem. This, then, is the second main reason that I wrote *NLD from the Inside Out*: to tell the world, "We're here, we're not going away, and neither is our NLD. Please learn to cope."

This brings me to the third reason for writing this book. Though we (NLDers and our parents) often have read, heard, or been told that all of the symptoms of NLD are permanent, my research has shown that this is not the case. While my book was and still is the first book about NLD to prove this with primary research, I understand that there is much more work to be done, as evidenced by the hundreds of responses I have received, in the original 2007 survey, from the many emails I received since then, and in the 2015 survey for this new edition.

Overall, I wrote this book because, like you (or your child or student), I have Nonverbal Learning Disabilities, or NLD. The other people in the book who tell their stories also have NLD. Most of us grew up and went all the way through school not knowing what was "wrong" with us. Some were diagnosed with "non-specified learning disabilities" because that's how we could get into Special Education (SPED) classes. Many did not get a correct diagnosis until our late teens or early 20s. I was 24, almost 25, when I first found out I had NLD, but I had been in SPED since first grade, after my teachers noticed that I was "different."

You'll hear more of my story, and those of others who grew up with NLD, who are now teens to young adults, in these pages.

We want your parents and teachers to know that you *are* trying hard, that your problems have a specific biological basis, and that consequently, you have to work *a lot* harder than most people, which is why you might get tired and frustrated often.

What you will see in *NLD from the Inside Out* is an amalgam of scholarly research and references, my own experiences and opinions, and most importantly, the experiences of many other young adults with NLD, who contributed narratives about their struggles, triumphs, feelings, observations, failures, challenges, and successes. When you see text in *italics*, those are direct quotes from the people I interviewed for this book, or from the people who answered either or both of the surveys. They have generously agreed to share their stories, advice, and wisdom with you, the reader.

I have tried to make the information in this book as relevant and up to date as possible, using some new information and research skills gained while earning my master's degree in 2009. Since August 2008, when the first edition was published, a lot has changed that affects NLDers. Since then, President Bush signed into law a revised version of the Americans with Disabilities Act. President Obama included in the Affordable Care Act of 2009 an overhaul of the way student loans are structured, as well as new insurance regulations, both of which affect many of us. In 2013, the American Psychiatric Association (APA) published the fifth edition of the Diagnostic and Statistical Manual of Mental Disorders (DSM-5). And in 2014,

Congress passed the Achieving a Better Life Experience (ABLE) Act, which allows families of people with disabilities to establish tax-free savings accounts. And that's just political change.

Neuroscience is advancing rapidly, with many exciting new findings, just in the past two years. New books on learning disabilities are continually being published. And yet, with as much attention as attention deficit disorder (ADD), autism, and Asperger's Syndrome have received, I still have yet to see one novel, movie, ribbon campaign, or "Awareness Day" that mentions NLD outright. Until that day comes, we need to be better informed than we were before.

Introduction

NLD from the Inside Out started out as a 15-page final paper for a psychology class I took in 2004 at Clark University in Worcester, Massachusetts. When I later decided to expand the paper into my senior thesis, I realized that not only did it need a lot more research, but it also needed some real street cred. So I found and interviewed five students with NLD, aged 17–24. I asked them 12 questions about what it was really like to have NLD, such as:

- "What has been the most frustrating for you in terms of having NLD?"

- "When did you first get the impression that you might be different?"

- "If you could tell your previous teachers one thing they should know about NLD, what would that be?"

The results amazed me: these NLD students, who ordinarily had such a hard time communicating their feelings (a common trait of NLD), who generally felt that no one could understand them, completely opened up to me as we talked, because I was a fellow "NLDer." Through talking with and observing them, I could tell that they really needed to be heard. And finally, someone was listening. They passionately expressed their wish to be acknowledged and to speak their minds about teachers and classes, and about how desperately they wanted their parents to understand them.

When I completed the thesis, and graduated with honors from Clark in May 2006, I realized that this research definitely was just the tip of the iceberg in getting the word out about what it was *really* like to live with NLD. I discussed this idea with my mother,

Gail Shapiro, who suggested that I expand the thesis into a book. The idea of writing a book was both daunting and exciting. I said I would do it if she would be the editor, because when one has NLD, project organization is a major challenge.

I wanted the book to be for teens with NLD, primarily because I wish I'd had a book like this while I was navigating adolescence, and I know my family and teachers could have used some guidance too. And who better to learn from than those who have made it past the horrors of high school and are now succeeding in college or in the workplace as young adults with NLD?

So I decided to find a way to reach people: both those with and without an official diagnosis of NLD, who were 18 to 30 years old at the time. I created a website,[1] and used SurveyMonkey™, an online survey instrument, to design and post a comprehensive survey with more than 80 questions about what it was like to have NLD.

At the same time, I joined four different online forums about NLD and other learning disabilities (LD). I posted my request for respondents on each of these boards, and the results were astounding! In addition to getting respondents, I got dozens of emails, most of them from desperate-sounding mothers of children with NLD, Asperger's Syndrome, or other learning disabilities. Many were confused and upset about their children, and thought I somehow had all the answers to their problems. Some even addressed me as "Professor Murphy," while others begged for referrals to psychologists, therapists, or schools where their children would be accepted and welcomed and would not be treated like freaks. In reading these emails, I felt overwhelmed and sad.

But it also made me realize that the work I was doing was important.

Amazingly, more than 100 people were both concerned and gracious enough to reply to the lengthy survey (if any of you are reading this—thanks again!), and I was able to use all the data from nearly 40 percent of these replies.

Although I thought I had run the gamut of topics to be covered, as soon as the first edition was published with BookLocker,[2] an independent print-on-demand publishing company, I again was flooded with emails from parents and NLDers seeking my advice on not just finding doctors and therapists, but also on dating and finding learning disability-friendly colleges, and asking me if I could advise them as to whether their NLD child should be on a certain medication. (To this last point: No. I am not a doctor, and I have neither taken, nor, for the most part, even heard of these medications, so I am not qualified to answer this question.) At various points, I have been asked to help students write papers on what it means to have NLD, to help parents craft Individualized Education Plans (IEPs), to speak in remote locations, and to conduct webinars, and I even have been asked to serve as an expert witness in a custody hearing. And while you can't please all the people all of the time, the second edition seemed to please most of the people most of the time, to the tune of reaching readers in 37 countries.

Still, for all this, I knew there was more work to be done and more questions to be answered, so I went back to the beginning. I reread the comments for the survey, and found that there were certain questions like, "Do NLDers stir the bubbles out of their soda?" or, "Are Aspies left handed and NLDers right handed?" that originally made me laugh. But now I thought these might need to be reevaluated to find the questions behind the questions. Eventually, I decided that I needed to create a new survey, and start over.

So here are the changes you will find in this third edition.

First, many sections have been expanded and reorganized. Each symptom of NLD is now more fully described, based on the latest discoveries in neuroscience. And I have responded to readers' most frequently asked questions, received since the first edition was published. In all, I hope you will find this edition of *NLD from the Inside Out* to be even more useful, more inspiring, and more informative than the first two.

Part I, "What Is NLD?" is devoted to explaining the nature of NLD. In Chapter One, you will read an overview of what a learning disability is and what NLD is. Chapter Two presents a short history of NLD, going back to the late 1960s when it was first named, as well as some theories about why it seems that today more kids than ever before may have NLD. Chapter Three gives a more in-depth discussion of the definition of NLD. Here you will learn about how to tell the difference between NLD and other learning disabilities, how NLD is diagnosed, and whether the diagnostic tests are really as fair and objective as they are designed to be. Finally, Chapter Three gives a symptom-by-symptom overview of the findings from the surveys and interviews conducted for this book.

In Part II, "The NLD Brain," Chapter Four presents an overview of what is actually going on inside your brain. In Chapters Five through Eight, the neurological basis of many of the most common NLD symptom areas are clarified and explained, namely: sensory sensitivities (Chapter Five), social cues and empathy (Chapter Six), executive functioning and decision-making (Chapter Seven), and specific learning disabilities (Chapter Eight). Because neuroscience is advancing so rapidly, some of this information may be out of date even by the time you read these chapters. Still, it offers you a new understanding of what can be gleaned about NLD from a scientific perspective.

Part III, "What We Want You to Know," presents several examples of the everyday stress of living with NLD, tells how this stress can lead to learned helplessness, discusses the fact that you are likely to become more resilient as you get older, and offers a glimpse into what life is really like for those of us with NLD, plus what NLDers need you to know. Chapter Nine is written for therapists and guidance counselors, Chapter Ten for teachers and school administrators, and Chapter Eleven for parents.

In Part IV, "Preparing for a Successful Life," dozens of young adults with NLD share advice about things that were frustrating and puzzling for us. We talk about how we addressed these problems, and tell you where we found some answers. In Chapter Twelve, you will read how to be more successful in high school. In Chapter Thirteen, you will learn how to succeed at dating and relationships. In Chapter Fourteen, you will learn tips for surviving and thriving in college, or whatever you choose to do right after high school. And in Chapter Fifteen, "It's a Wonderful Life—Even with NLD," you will hear what we consider to be the elements of a good life, plus what we wish we'd known earlier, and what we NLDers want you to know now— to give you a head start on making your life better.

Finally Part V, "The Big Questions," discusses why NLD is still given short shrift as a learning disability, and often doesn't count as a "real" diagnosis, and what you can do about it.

I hope that you will read this book and share it with your parents, your teachers, your therapist and doctors, your siblings, aunts, uncles, and cousins, your friends, neighbors, and religious leaders, and anyone else who you think would benefit from an explanation of NLD. My goal is that every one of these people in your life—including you—will better understand what it is like to have NLD, and will learn how to help you grow to be the best person you can be.

Part I

What Is NLD?

Chapter One

What Is NLD?

I was always a curious child. When I was two, I cut open my sister's feather pillow to see how many feathers were in it. I wasn't trying to make trouble; I wanted to make sense of the world. I taught myself to read at age three, and especially liked to read about Curious George™. One day, when no one was paying much attention, I went to the laundry room, and got the big box of soap powder and dumped it in the middle of the living room floor. Then I went outside to get the hose, and turned it on, and was on my way back so I could make lots and lots of bubbles, just like Curious George™. I got caught, and I had to clean up the soap powder. And I was sent to my room.

Being sent to their rooms rarely, if ever, has the desired effect on NLD kids. For most of us, it's a treat, not a punishment. But back then, we didn't know that I had NLD. Here's what my parents and preschool teachers knew: I was smart and curious, could read and spell, and had an extensive vocabulary. I couldn't ride a tricycle until I was about five. I didn't learn to ride a two-wheeler until I was nine. I was kind of a klutz athletically, and even today, my fine and gross motor skills aren't as good as those of my peers.

I started out doing fine academically, but by about the time I got to the fourth grade, when papers were assigned, I couldn't keep up. I would get an assignment to write an essay, or even a paragraph, and I might get the first few words down, and then I would just stare at the paper. I could not write a paper until I got to college. Actually, it wasn't until I got to my third college that I really learned how to write a paper. (I attended four different colleges before earning my bachelor's degree.)

By this time, I had received a diagnosis of "Learning Disability—Not Otherwise Specified" (LD—NOS), but this wasn't much better. So I decided to find out what it was.

The meaning of a learning disability

In order to understand Nonverbal Learning Disabilities (NLD), it's helpful first to understand what a "learning disability" is. According to most clinical definitions, it's a set of symptoms, each of which is based on a neurological impairment—either genetically inherited or trauma induced—so that the total effect of all symptoms has a negative effect on your ability to perform at least as well as your peers in some aspects: academically, socially, and/or physically.

A learning disability (LD) may hinder your ability to learn or to perform a skill: not understanding what the skill is, not understanding how to perform it, not being able to perform it, not understanding the logic behind the "rules" of the skill, or perhaps not understanding the reason for it at all.

Since the mid-1990s, there has been much controversy over what the "D" in "LD" stands for. Today, many people—professionals and laypeople alike—may refer to "learning differences," "learning disorders," or even "learning disease"!

Clearly, to say that you have a "learning disease" is both counterproductive and counterintuitive. To say that there is a disease from which you suffer is to say that you are sick (and that possibly you could get better or could somehow be contagious), which is not helpful at all and entirely misleading. Moreover, the nomenclature of the term "disease" might lead others to assume that you need medication or treatment.

But what is wrong with saying that "LD" stands for "learning differences?" That seems harmless enough. Every one of us learns differently from one another, just as each person has his or her own unique personality. Vocational rehabilitation counselor Joyanne Cobb, founder of the Professionals with Disabilities Resource Network, puts it this way: "If we only say that we are people who learn *differently*, then we are also saying that we are not *disabled*. In that case, legislation on accommodations for the disabled no longer apply to us."[3] And growing up with NLD, you need to know your rights—

both in school and college, and in the workplace. The Individuals with Disabilities Education Act (IDEA) ensures accommodations and an Individualized Education Plan (IEP) for students with disabilities, just as the Americans with Disabilities Act (ADA) protects people in the workforce who have a documented disability, but there is no legislation that protects you if you simply refer to yourself as "different."

> *One thing I've wondered is: who gets to say what a disability is, anyway, and what is "normal?"*

What of other "D words" that might serve as a substitute for "disability"? It would be nice if the "D" in "LD" stood not for "disabilities" or "differences," but "difficulties." Yet even then, who's to say that dealing with your difficulties is any more pressing than dealing with anybody else's difficulties? Perhaps the best term would be "learning disorders." That way, all that is implied is that, yes, you have a disorder, so there's something a little "disorderly" about your patterns of behavior vis-à-vis learning, but there's no real expectation that you can't learn (either now or ever), nor is there an expectation to think that whatever is disorderly cannot be made (more) orderly—something you will see in the latter chapters of this book. So why "learning disability" instead of "learning disorder"? Again, it comes back to the legal issue. In neither the ADA nor the IDEA does the "D" stand for "disorder." You will learn more about this in Chapter Sixteen.

The term "learning disability" does not properly reflect the fact that if you have a learning disability, you simply learn differently from non-LD people. And while the term "disability" doesn't necessarily imply that you can't learn—in which case we would use the term "inability" instead—labeling it a "disability" sounds as though you once had the ability, but were rendered inoperative. It appears to put the blame on external factors, rather than dealing with the fact that here is a child who has trouble with writing, reading, social skills, etc., and who needs help.

In this book, the term "Nonverbal Learning Disabilities" (without hyphenating "Nonverbal," or saying "Disability" in the singular or "Disorder," and not including the "V" as in "NVLD") will be used, simply because it is the most widely recognized and accepted nomenclature. You also will see the word "neurotypical," a term originating in the autism community to mean "not autistic," and which, for the purpose of this book, loosely means both, "not having gone through Special Education," as well as, "not exhibiting most of the symptoms of NLD."

How can you recognize NLD?

Does this sound like you?

- You began to read on your own at a very early age.

- You astonished your parents and elementary school teachers with your advanced vocabulary.

- You didn't learn to ride a bike until you were eight or nine, and you may have been clumsy in both gross and fine motor skills.

- You've had a parent or teacher refuse to acknowledge that anything is the matter other than your own laziness, lack of trying, ineptitude, or bad attitude.

- You've had a parent or sibling who "babied" you.

- You've had teachers who threw up their hands in frustration, telling your parents, "I just can't get through to him/her."

- You've been labeled as a "discipline problem" in school—maybe not for serious stuff, but for the stuff that gets attention.

- You've had teachers ask, "You are so bright—why aren't you working up to your potential?"

- You've sat and stared at a writing assignment for English class, unable to get past writing the first sentence or two.

- You may have no or only a couple of friends; other kids see you as nerdy or uncool.

- You get along much better with adults than with your peers.

- If you are a young adult, you may be unemployed or under-employed, because you have been unable to find a work environment that matches your skills and strengths.

- You suffer from depression, low self-esteem, or loneliness, but are developing coping skills as you grow up.

Or does the above list sound like your child? If so, maybe the following points apply.

- You have wondered why he/she is so bright, yet so immature.

- You often worry about your child's safety and well-being, with each age bringing a new set of concerns.

- You have spent hours in teacher conferences, discussing IEPs and other strategies for classroom success.

- You have (or would like to be able to) quit your job, in order to devote more time to your child, *or*:

  o you (or your spouse) are in complete denial about your child's disabilities, and think that he or she should just try harder and "buckle down."

- You have argued with your spouse about the "right" way to discipline this nonconforming child.

- You feel you are neglecting your other children and your spouse, because this child takes so much of your time and energy.

- You live with a constant high level of stress and anxiety, which may translate into physical and/or emotional health issues.

- You often feel like a failure. You wonder what you might have done to cause the disability and you lie awake at night, wondering how you can be a better parent.

If you can identify with either of these lists, or if you teach or work with families who can, read on.

The NLD "syndrome"

A classic example of how NLD manifests, familiar to many children, is Amelia Bedelia, a lovable character created in 1963 by the late children's author Peggy Parish. Literal to the point of silliness, Amelia Bedelia, a housekeeper who works for Mr. and Mrs. Rogers, tries to be helpful, as she follows her employers' instructions exactly. For example, when told to "dust the furniture," she sprinkles the furniture with dust. When asked to "draw the drapes," she gets out her pencil and paper and starts sketching. Every little kid with NLD can relate to this, and so can most parents.

But what exactly is NLD?

Nonverbal Learning Disabilities gets its name from the fact that our major language functions, such as reading and verbal output, are not usually affected, in contrast to most other language-based learning disabilities. Those of us with NLD often are characterized as "excellent" in certain academic areas such as spelling and grammar rules, history, geography, physical sciences, some standardized tests, and in most areas that require logic and memorization. However, we may do poorly when it comes to English and social science courses, where written papers are required, as many of us tend to be deficient in executive functioning skills. This means that we may have trouble with prioritization, impulse control, attention, retention, and organization. The lack of ability to plan, to organize work, and to foresee consequences are common symptoms of NLD.

> I'm not really sure what my problems are, but my bag's so messy, and my handwriting's horrible, and…they're a little tough to deal with.

> I'm never exactly sure what to do in a new situation. It seems like everyone else does, but I don't see how they figure it out without asking.

A very hard question for us NLDers to answer is, "Why is this particular action the correct thing to do in this situation?" We often have an excellent, extensive vocabulary, and good rote memory skills, pay great attention to detail, and are early readers. However, other language-based tasks often are a challenge. For some with NLD, especially females, math is the biggest challenge.

Simply put, NLD is unlike many of the better-publicized learning disabilities such as dyslexia and attention deficit hyperactivity disorder (ADHD), as NLD has no one identifiable specific problem focus, such as difficulty with reading, distractibility, and/or hyperactivity. Instead, the neuropsychological methods of diagnosing NLD employ examining what amounts to a laundry list of symptoms.

Individuals with NLD are not stubborn, spoiled, lazy slackers—as many of those who interact with us might believe. NLD is caused by deficiencies or damage to the brain, as you will learn in Chapters Four through Eight.

Lynda Katz, former president of Landmark College in Putney, Vermont, a two-year school for students with learning disabilities, and her co-authors state that the definition of NLD usually reflects "the perspective of the professionals involved"[4]—that is, teachers, doctors, school administrators, therapists, and others each define NLD through their particular lens.

As it stands, there is no general consensus as to one specific, definitive way to identify, diagnose, or treat NLD. Because this is the case, it is vitally important to *listen to the voices of NLDers themselves*, so we can come to a much better understanding of what NLD is and how it operates.

So, how was NLD "discovered"? How many people have NLD? How did "Nonverbal Learning Disabilities" become an official diagnosis, and how did its relevant terminology develop? Read on.

Chapter Two
A Short History of NLD

In 1967, Northwestern University researchers Doris Johnson and Helmer Mykelbust coined the term "nonverbal disorders of learning," which quickly evolved into "nonverbal learning disabilities" to refer to students who did not have a "verbal learning disability," but who were not performing up to par in school, and therefore should be viewed as having a "disorder of social imperception."[5] To Johnson and Mykelbust, "nonverbal" learning disorders could be divided into two categories: "Nonsocial–Nonverbal" and "Social–Nonverbal."[6] At the time, other researchers were also looking into specific learning disabilities from a psychological perspective, and still others from a neurological perspective, but it was Johnson and Mykelbust (especially Mykelbust) who saw the need for these two fields to inform each other.[7]

Though the concept of a "nonverbal learning disability" was widely rejected by educators and psychologists throughout the 1970s and early to mid-1980s, some were doing research to find out the root of the impairments to the brain that would comprise this "disorder of social imperception." By comparing the overall combination of these symptoms to those found in other neuropsychological disorders due to brain lesions and trauma, the general consensus by the mid-1980s was that what Johnson and Mykelbust described amounted to a disorder specific to the right hemisphere of the brain.

The late Canadian researcher Byron P. Rourke is considered to be the first psychologist to identify what we know today as NLD. His research and books became the veritable bible of NLD information, and until as recently as a few years ago, many of the books about NLD by both parents and psychologists simply cited his research.

In his 1989 book *Nonverbal Learning Disabilities: The Syndrome and the Model*,[8] Rourke described the history of the concept of a learning disability, which he said was first discovered in the 1970s, when he and his colleagues began to notice children who were not as "normal" as others. These children were given the Wechsler Intelligence Scale for Children® (WISC)[9] and divided into subgroups according to the gap between their Verbal IQ (intelligence quotient) and Performance IQ scores (these will be explained later).

Those whose Performance score was more than ten points higher than their Verbal score were labeled "Group RS" to indicate poor performance in Reading and Spelling as the most prominent discrepancy. Those whose IQ differential was ten points or fewer in either direction were labeled "Group RSA," as they were shown to have equal deficits in the areas of Reading, Spelling, and Arithmetic. Those whose Verbal IQ scores were more than ten points higher than their Performance IQ scores were labeled "Group A," to indicate poor performance in Arithmetic as the most prominent, but not the only, discrepancy.[10]

Rourke also posited that all those right-hemisphere neurological impairments that contributed to the problems in socio-emotional reasoning in the child with a "disorder of social imperception" were identical to those neurological impairments that contributed to the problems in mathematical reasoning. In other words, according to Rourke, in terms of forming the definition of "Nonverbal Learning Disabilities," difficulties in socio-emotional reasoning and difficulties in mathematical reasoning were inseparable. This was why all the "Group A" children had NLD, even though Johnson and Mykelbust contended that although most to all of their students with mathematical disorders had difficulties with socio-emotional reasoning, the converse was not necessarily true.

In addition, Rourke contributed the ideas that the Verbal IQ must be at least ten points higher than the Performance IQ in order for there to be a diagnosis of NLD, and that the brain-based cause of NLD was due to a deficit of white matter (which will be explained in Chapter Four).[11] This was the precedent set back in 1989.

Beginning in the late 1990s, as NLD became more recognizable, many books were written by teachers and parents of children with NLD: that is, NLD as previously defined by Rourke. Pioneers such as

Pamela Tanguay,[12] Sue Thompson,[13] Katherine Stewart,[14] and others began to redefine what NLD really was, based on the behavior of their children and students.

In so doing, suddenly the floodgates burst open, introducing parents of NLDers, as well as lay readers, to a whole new set of terms such as "executive functioning," "metacognition," "hard/soft signs," and others, as well as many comparisons of NLD to other learning disabilities. Parents, teachers, and school administrators began to take NLD seriously, and to create IEPs for NLD students.

New clinical information and theories of NLD have been put forth more recently.

In his 2006 book, *Nonverbal Learning Disabilities: A Clinical Perspective*,[15] clinical social worker Joseph Palombo radically revamped the definition of NLD with his "Theory of NLD Subtypes." According to Palombo, there exists a core of Nonlinguistic Perceptual Deficits—a set of symptoms of NLD common to everyone who has it. This set of deficits, he says, constitutes "NLD Subtype I." If, in addition to meeting the criteria for NLD Subtype I, you also have difficulties in attention, impulse control, and executive functioning, you fall into the category of "NLD Subtype II." Or if, in addition to meeting the requirements for NLD Subtype I, you have difficulties in "reciprocal social interactions" (e.g. being argumentative, being disrespectful, having few or no close friends, and/or being teased and rejected by peers), "social communication difficulties" (e.g. not knowing what and what not to say, and when and when not to say it), and "emotional functioning difficulties" (e.g. poor self-esteem, anxiety, and poor self-regulation), to the exclusion of having problems with attention, impulse control, and executive functioning, then you have "NLD Subtype III." If, however, you meet *all* the criteria, then you have "NLD Subtype IV."[16]

Psychologist Maggie Mamen divides NLD into four distinct areas: Perceptual NLD, Social NLD, Written Expressive NLD, and Attentional NLD in her 2007 book, *Understanding Nonverbal Learning Disabilities: A Common-Sense Guide for Parents and Professionals*. And in their 2011 book, *Nonverbal Learning Disabilities in Children: Bridging the Gap Between Science and Practice*, written primarily for school-based professionals, psychologist and professor John M. Davis and psychoanalyst Jessica Broitman discuss the nuances and history of defining NLD, subtypes, and neurology.

There are many books about NLD, written either by doctors or psychologists, or parents of kids with NLD. Most of these writers examine NLD through the lens of their own child, their own clients, or their own patients, but they don't get it, at least not completely. You need to live with NLD to really get it. No matter how tough life may be for you right now, you are not likely to feel that way forever. We learned to deal with our NLD, and so will you.

Are there more people with NLD today than there used to be?

When the NLD syndrome was first identified by Rourke in 1989, he estimated that, although 8 percent of U.S. schoolchildren were enrolled in SPED classes for a learning disability, only 10 percent of all children with learning disabilities had NLD, up from 5 percent in 1968. Or to put it another way, about one of every 100 students had NLD; further, he said this number was equally distributed between males and females, up from five boys for every girl.[17] However, it is not sufficiently clear that this estimated ratio is or ever was correct. For example, the interviews and two surveys for this book show a ratio of 69 percent female to 31 percent male.

Most of the current literature about NLD—much of which still cites Rourke—states that the prevalence of NLD is about 1 percent of the general population (the given range is from 0.5% to 1.5%), or about 10 percent of those identified as having a learning disability, both as defined by Rourke, and as defined by more current measures.

According to the United States Census Bureau, as of December 2015, there were 87,979,043 children, aged 0 to 19. A 2014 study by the National Center for Learning Disabilities[18] states that 2.4 million American public school students (approximately 5% of the total public school enrollment) are identified with learning disabilities, and that an additional 15 percent or more of students "struggle due to unidentified and unaddressed learning and attention issues." Another 10 percent of children, or about 240,000, attend private schools or are homeschooled.

So the real implication of these data is this: it is likely that between 879,790 (1% of the general population) and 960,000 (10% of those with both diagnosed and undiagnosed learning disabilities) U.S. children ages 19 and younger have NLD, and that the total number of children and adults is close to 3 million.

Whatever the incidence or prevalence may actually be, it is increasingly important for more people to understand NLD. As one interviewee explains:

> Even though 99 percent of the population does not have NLD, they will at some point meet, befriend, study with, teach, marry, give birth to, advise, work next to, supervise, or otherwise interact with an NLD individual.

Why does NLD seem to be so much more prevalent today than it was in our parents' or grandparents' generations, when no one had ever heard of it? Why are there still so many new cases of NLD diagnosed each year? Of the many different theories and ideas about the causes of NLD, perhaps the best can be attributed to Rondalyn Whitney, founder of the Lighthouse Project.[19]

Whitney presented three main reasons: one of which may be an actual cause; another one, a reason for the increase in the prevalence of NLD; and the third, a reason why we are noticing more people with NLD than ever before.

The first is genetic. The DNA of an NLD individual contains an accumulation of at least some of the visual–spatial, social relationship, mathematical, and other deficiencies characteristic of each parent. One partial disability concurrent with another results in a greater chance of NLD in the offspring of two such individuals.

Whitney's second theory was that NLD is the result of environmental toxins, such as overuse of computers, effects of late-life pregnancies, and high-stress lifestyles. But the third—the lack of opportunities to develop motor and social skills as part of everyday play—was the theory to which Whitney gave the most credibility. Writing in 2002, she explained that "30 years ago," most children "ran and rode bikes from morning till sundown. They explored in the woods and climbed trees for hours…" They had many more opportunities to develop their social skills, as well as "visual, proprioceptive, vestibular and tactile experience[s]."[20]

Back in around 1970, the period to which Whitney refers, there was no system of SPED classes. Those who had NLD symptoms may have struggled, but they were expected to keep up with the class. All students learned handwriting using the Palmer Method, in which cursive writing was taught using rhythmic motions. In English classes, there was no "creative" writing ("creative" meaning "just express your feelings and don't worry about punctuation, spelling, or grammar"). Spelling was taught by rote and students learned to diagram sentences. These highly structured teaching techniques were very, very helpful to students with NLD. And their use may have helped greatly to ameliorate some students' NLD symptoms.

So it seems that the recent increase in NLD diagnoses may be the result of lifestyle changes and teaching techniques that do not give children sufficient opportunity to develop fully their fine and gross motor skills, planning skills, or social skills.

Still, it is important to note that the 1 percent figure was first put forth in 1989, and no one has proven or disproven it since— nor, it seems, even questioned it. This also is true with the statistic commonly cited that of all those with learning disabilities, 10 percent have NLD. But even that's an estimate; no one actually has real data.

Part of the problem in determining this number is that, because the United States Census Bureau's definitions of the different types of disabilities do not include NLD, there can be no statistics on it. Another problem is the ever shifting and renaming of disorders according to the APA's Diagnostic and Statistical Manual of Mental Disorders (DSM), about which you will learn more in Chapter Sixteen.

And if the reported rates of both ADHD and Autism Spectrum Disorders (ASD) are on the rise, it is possible that NLD is getting squeezed out—and being replaced by those more common, and medically defined, disorders. So maybe the only real way to report how many NLDers there are is to count the number of people who self-identify as having it.

How do you know whether you have NLD, if you have not yet been tested, or if your test results were inconclusive? The next chapter may give you some answers.

Chapter Three

Diagnosing NLD

I just wish that when I had been tested, either in sixth grade or eighth grade, the two times I was tested, that there had been some diagnosis, not just: "this is what needs to happen in your school right now," but also: "this is WHY this needs to happen. This is the diagnosis and this is what's up with your brain." And to have someone [to] have explained it to me then.

If your first diagnosis is a correct one, you can avoid years of mislabeling, misinformation, and not getting the right interventions to help you succeed both educationally and socially. But if you may have been diagnosed with NLD, or you or your parents think you may have it, but you don't know for sure, how can you find out? The answer isn't that simple. NLD can be very difficult to diagnose, for several reasons. The survey asked, "What, if anything, got in the way of your being diagnosed with NLD?" The answers seemed to fall into a few clusters.

1: We were diagnosed too young

[I was] tested at age 10, no learning disability indicated. LD was mistaken for lack of effort.

I was diagnosed fairly young at age 12. I first was assessed at about the age of six or seven and was not given a diagnosis of NLD but I'm not sure of the cause of that or the results of that assessment. I am fairly sure that some learning difficulties were determined in that earliest assessment.

Everybody just thought I was weird and a troublemaker/class clown-type. They did not look for a learning disability at all.

In addition, the survey asked, "How old were you when you first were diagnosed correctly, and who did the diagnosis?" As diagnostics tests have improved and there is more general awareness now about NLD, diagnostic times are younger. The respondents said:

25, neuropsychologist. (Male, age 30)

I was 21 before they figured it out. I went to a psychologist who missed the diagnosis, then to a neuropsych specialist who got it. (Male, age 27)

Age 17, neuropsychologist. (Female, age 22)

I was 12 when I was first accurately diagnosed by a private doctor. My parents took me to be tested because I was having trouble with handwriting and because of ongoing bullying issues and social anxiety. (Male, age 19)

11 years old, school psychologist. (Male, age 21)

Age 11 and again at age 25. (Female, age 25)

2: No one "got it"

Another group said that their early tests showed that "something was wrong," but no one seemed to know what it was:

…until very recently, none of the people who diagnosed me had a name for it. Nobody—teachers, parents, counselors, and school psychologists— knew about NLD.

[They] put me in classes that I didn't belong in (Special Ed).

IGNORANCE.

Nobody knew about it (NLD) at the time. My psychiatrist was more concerned with giving me a lot of medication than with diagnosing me and getting treatment.

In addition, several of the respondents know or are pretty sure they have NLD, but have yet to receive a correct diagnosis. The survey asked, "If [you have not received a] diagnosis, what makes you think you have NLD?" They said:

A neuropsychologist that I went to for years told me that it was very likely that I had NLD, but that at that time (1997), there was no way of officially diagnosing me in the Netherlands (where I live). Also, if diagnosed, I would be obliged to tell employers. This is why I never asked for an official diagnosis later.

Everyone just thought I was weird, because I can read and write well. No one even looked for a learning disability.

I actually wasn't ever officially diagnosed. I was tested but not diagnosed with anything when I was in middle school. I was tested twice, in fact. But I didn't have a name for what I might have until I got to college.

3: We may be doing well

The diagnosis may be missed simply because we seem to be doing so well.

I was able to compensate so well as a child and teenager that no one would have guessed if they were speaking to me that I had a disability. I could verbally make sure people knew that I understood the material being presented.

I always got As and Bs throughout school, but when I went away to college, I started failing and couldn't handle being away from home, adjusting to college, meeting people and 12 credits of school work.

[…]But, I'm also glad that [my parents] didn't know about my NLD, because they pushed me further than I ever would have gotten if they had known about my diagnosis earlier.

4: Competing family priorities

Sometimes we—and our diagnosis—may get overlooked because of competing family priorities. That is, our parents also have to deal with our siblings, each other, and other family members. Our parents have their own problems. And they may be in denial that anything is wrong with us, or they may not agree with each other.

Nobody knew how big of a thing the social component was, and parents/ testers/teachers did not communicate with each other or do research. The school system should have, under the law, done a LOT more than they did. Also, my parents were busy being divorced and had other kids to worry about. I was quiet, got halfway decent grades, so nobody noticed I didn't make eye contact, y'know?

My parents didn't like me being seen by people they didn't know, didn't really believe in medical professionals. They thought I would grow out of it. By the time I was an adult, I was a functioning illiterate who barely graduated high school. Getting help was near impossible when you don't know what's wrong with you and you can't communicate with new people.

My father just blamed my mother for babying me, like my NLD was all her fault. Until I was 22, he would tell me I had to try to "act normal."

5: NLD often coexists with another diagnosis

The majority of the individuals interviewed for this book have had diagnoses of both NLD and something else, and the NLD usually takes a back seat to the other diagnosis. As a result, both of the diagnoses may be misunderstood.

Most of my disabilities were attributed to early emotional trauma. Once I was treated and the symptoms persisted, it was dyslexia, then ADD. None of these explained the savant-like verbal skills, social isolation, or the crippling sensitivity to touch, among others.

I was very quiet and did not cause problems so I was easy to overlook. I was also very depressed from about 14 on, so some of my NLD symptoms were mistaken for depression.

[What got in the way of a correct diagnosis was] that my EEGs are abnormal. People thought I had epilepsy for years.

ADHD, ODD [oppositional defiant disorder]. Both diagnoses were thrown out after testing.

In elementary school or middle school, I was diagnosed as ADD. In high school, evaluation ruled out ADD and diagnosed a learning disability of "unspecified type." Also I have a psychiatric history of depression and anxiety.

Asperger's Syndrome.

I don't remember most of them, but a few: slow processing speed, executive functioning disorder, motor disorder.

Age 18, I got a diagnosis of LD—NOS. At age 22, I was diagnosed with social-emotional processing disorder, but I've had epilepsy my entire life.

Suspicion of ADHD in early education, the school asked to have testing done but my family declined because characteristics didn't seem to fit.

Originally PDD—NOS [pervasive developmental disorder—not otherwise specified], then NLD, and recently switched to a primary diagnosis of ASD for the purposes of the latest DSM.

Bipolar disorder, changed to Asperger's Syndrome.

What are some of the other disorders that may be confused with, masquerade as, or coexist with NLD, making the NLD diagnosis difficult or impossible? ADD and Autism Spectrum Disorder (which now includes what used to be called "Asperger's Syndrome") are two of the closest diagnoses to NLD.

NLD and ADD

I was not diagnosed with NLD, but as having a personality "like ADD."

As I look back over the years I have realized that my ADD tendencies could be traced back to NLD. For instance, I was always disorganized, often forgot homework assignments, had difficulty paying attention, and took a long time learning simple things such as basic math concepts and the difference between left and right. But there were many other symptoms that were too obviously different from ADD that I could not possibly be diagnosed with it; I was lacking in the hyperactivity aspect of ADD, and I always thought things through before I did them, so I have come to a self-diagnosis of NLD.

Because it is so well-known, ADD might be considered the "king of learning disabilities." No other learning disability is diagnosed as frequently, has had as many "quick fixes" thought up for it, has had as much media hype, or is talked about as colloquially (e.g. "she's totally ADD"). And its very predominance is exactly what provides cause for so much misunderstanding about what NLD is. We all (think we) know what ADD looks like: poor short-term memory, impulse control, organization, and focus, with hyperactivity optional. So, essentially, it seems, ADD is a matter of poor executive functioning skills.

What is the difference between ADD and NLD? ADD is thought to be characterized "only" by executive functioning problems, with none of the other NLD symptoms. What happens if you have both ADD and dysgraphia? Then you just have ADD and sloppy handwriting. But what if, in addition to the ADD and dysgraphia, you also have poor social skills? Where is the line drawn to say that it's no longer ADD, but now NLD?

The predominance of ADD diagnoses makes it more difficult to diagnose NLD. What otherwise might be diagnosed outright as NLD, thus providing a broader definition and hence awareness of NLD, or as "NLD *minus* symptom A, B, or C," often is diagnosed instead as "ADD *plus* symptom A, B, or C."

NLD and Asperger's

A large part of the misunderstanding lies in the fact that there are different standards of definition, and hence different methods of diagnosis. Whereas a neuropsychologist might arrive at a diagnosis of NLD by analyzing the results of a diagnostic test such as the WISC, he or she could arrive at a diagnosis of ADD or Autism Spectrum Disorder by determining that the subject displays the symptoms listed in the DSM.

Often, both we and our parents are asked, "Isn't NLD just a mild form of Asperger's Syndrome (AS)?" The experts don't agree. As of this writing, NLD is still categorized as a learning disability, while Asperger's Syndrome, once officially categorized by the APA as a mental illness in the DSM-IV-TR, has since been dropped from the DSM-5 (yes, the APA just switched from Roman to Arabic numerals with this edition) and replaced (and, one could say, subsumed) by the term Autism Spectrum Disorder.

NLD and Williams Syndrome

Another disorder that shares symptoms with NLD is Williams Syndrome. While those with NLD normally have IQs much higher than those with Williams Syndrome, there are striking similarities between the two. Elementary-school-aged NLD children may have difficulty in age-appropriate math skills, and difficulty in tying their shoelaces. The latter can be explained by Sue Thompson's description that motor skills are the main means for comparability. Both NLD and Williams Syndrome are thought to share a common flaw on one gene in chromosome #7.[21] Exactly 25 genes out of 30,000 are missing in Williams, while the ones responsible for the cognitive and social effects number three to six—the symptoms of which are characterized by "significant gross, fine, and visual-motor problems; [and] dysgraphia."[22]

Moreover, for someone with Williams, as with NLD, there is a tendency not only to miss social cues, but also to be overly friendly and trusting, having no qualms about befriending strangers.

Many of these Williams Syndrome symptoms overlap with those that define NLD, and incidentally are the same symptoms that differentiate NLD from Autism Spectrum Disorders. Not being a clinician, I cannot theorize about any causal relationship, but will suggest that the connection between NLD and Williams needs to be examined further.

6: Diagnostic tests may be flawed or biased

Perhaps the primary reason that NLD has been so hard to diagnose until very recently was due to several flaws and biases in the most common diagnostic tests. How did these flaws and biases develop, and what do they mean for us?

Diagnostic tests have been around for centuries. Harvard Professor Howard Gardner[23] describes the unique definitions of intelligence of various ancient cultures, such as the Confucian Chinese and Greeks. According to Gardner, a desire to understand a more common definition of intelligence has evolved over time. Intelligence tests evolved as a well-intentioned attempt to measure a person's intelligence, though because there are so many differences among people, IQ tests tend to fail miserably.

Gardner discusses how British polymath scientist Francis Galton and his cousin Charles Darwin undertook the first steps to create ways to measure intelligence, how testing was later refined by French psychologist Alfred Binet, and how still later developments such as the Scholastic Aptitude Test (SAT) or the WISC, described below, became the standard approach to understanding intelligence.

In 1939, psychologist David Wechsler designed a new model for measuring intelligence, separate from the previously existing Stanford-Binet test, which would include a much wider array of subtests, and thus more accurately determine one's IQ. At the time that he designed it, it was termed the Wechsler-Bellevue Intelligence Scale®. However, by 1955, he had created two other tests designed for children: the Wechsler Pre-school and Primary Scale of Intelligence® (WPPSI), designed for young children aged three to seven, and the Wechsler Intelligence Scale for Children® (WISC), for those seven to sixteen years old.

When these tests were created, the need arose to rename the Wechsler-Bellevue®, and so the main test was labeled the Wechsler Adult Intelligence Scale® (WAIS). In 1981, the WAIS® was revised, and the subsequent version came to be known as the WAIS-R®. And in 1997, another version, the WAIS-III®, came into use.[24] Similarly, the WISC® continued to be updated periodically, and the WISC-III® was published in 1991.

The significance of this information is that most of those interviewed or surveyed for this book were diagnosed using the WISC-III®. (Some who are younger, as well as many of you readers may have been diagnosed using the WISC-IV®, which came out in 2003.)

The WISC-III® test includes two sections, Verbal IQ and Performance IQ, and each section contains several subtests. The Verbal IQ subtests include: Information, Digit Span, Vocabulary, Arithmetic, Comprehension, and Similarities. The Performance IQ subtests are: Completion, Picture Arrangement, Block Design, Coding, Symbol Search, and Mazes.[25] In addition, the WISC-III®, like most other Wechsler tests, has four separate indices measuring verbal comprehension, perceptual organization, working memory, and processing speed.

The most important thing about the Wechsler tests is the way that they measure IQ. In each test result, there are three IQ scores given: a Verbal IQ (VIQ), a Performance IQ (PIQ), and a full-scale IQ. Each of the three separate IQs was set to record 100 points as the mean IQ, with a standard deviation of 15 points. What this means is that while someone may have had an overall full-scale IQ of 100 points, they may have scored, for example, 110 on the Verbal and 90 on the Performance section. So, while the (mean) full-scale IQ would be 100, the 20-point discrepancy would be significant enough to suggest that the test-taker had a learning disability.

Such discrepancies between VIQ and PIQ indeed have been indicative of learning disabilities. In 1989, Rourke summarized what were then considered to be the objectively observable assets and deficits that constitute NLD, and hypothesized that the VIQ>PIQ gap would only increase with age. Additionally, he pointed out brain traumas and factors other than genetics that would account for later onset NLD, after an individual has lived with a "normal" brain for most of his or her life. Ever since Rourke designated the "Group A" children as having NLD, it became generally accepted by test administrators that NLD (once it was titled as such) could be defined as the major discrepancy of VIQ being higher than PIQ.[26]

Why might this have been the case? For one thing, one of the most consistent indicators of NLD is that we have good to extremely good vocabularies. We also, as a rule, have below-average motor skills. However, it is just as important, if not more so, to note which specific weaknesses in the subtests were the basis for the discrepancy.

Even though Rourke proposed in 1989 that this point spread would only stay the same or increase over time, more recent research has shown that this may not be the case at all. In fact, the gap between the VIQ and PIQ scores may even decrease. In a 1999 article, NLD advocate and activist Pamela Tanguay describes to Rourke the problem she had with understanding her daughter's narrowing gap between her VIQ and PIQ scores:

> Although he personally answered my question, more importantly he clarified the issue from the podium next afternoon at a conference. His answer? The VIQ>PIQ profile, although common, is not always present, since the verbal score may be suppressed by the comprehension and arithmetic subtest scores. EUREKA!!![27]

Indeed, these two subtests, Comprehension and Arithmetic, were very problematic for NLD students, especially the Comprehension. The Comprehension subtest was described as, "16 questions in the form of 'Why do we _____?' or 'What should you do if _____?'

to test understanding of common-sense reasoning and social understanding."[28]

In other words, what was being tested was a knowledge of the ability to understand social cues and morals specific to the culture in which the test was being given. More to the point, it tested understanding of social norms relative to the culture of those who designed the test. Because the designers tended to be white, upper-middle class, well-educated males, this might explain why for so long the tests appeared to be biased against women, Black people, Hispanic people, and other minority groups. What, then, is the message one gets from being marked wrong, either because the test-taker didn't understand how to answer the question or realized that there really could not be any truly "correct" answer?

> *In kindergarten, they gave me an IQ test, and the tester asked me the opposite of "thin." I said "viscous." Wrong. You know, anyone at that age would have said that it was "thick" or "fat." But it just so happened that I'd been talking with my uncle the night before, and he was explaining the properties of oil, and he said it could range from very thin and watery to very viscous. So, my "wrong" answer was indicative of a low IQ.*

This problem also was noticeable in the PIQ Picture Arrangement subtest. If, in taking the test, you put the four picture tiles in the "wrong" order, yet it seemed logical to you, and you could explain to the administrator why it was logical to you, would it then be fair to say that these subtests were really valid? Or were they ultimately subjective? If these subtests were not valid, what could have been used to distinguish a lack in social understanding?

So, this simply begs the question: Do the VIQ and PIQ really help explain what they are meant to? Why, for example, is Arithmetic included in the Verbal section? Alan S. Kaufman discusses how there are really seven aspects of intelligence being tested in the WISC-III®: reasoning (arithmetic and object assembly), short-term memory (digit span and coding), long-term memory (information and picture completion), social understanding (comprehension and picture arrangement), concept formation (vocabulary and block design), verbal mediation (similarities and picture arrangement), and speed of processing (arithmetic and symbol search).[29]

What this means is that weaknesses in the PIQ subtest of picture arrangement counted as a double whammy in terms of both verbal mediation and social understanding, while every PIQ subtest tested for processing speed. At the same time, the strengths that could be shown in verbal comprehension were not limited to the VIQ subtests. And even though comprehension is the predominant indicator of NLD, there was only one VIQ subtest that could have put an NLDer in double jeopardy: arithmetic. So, back to Tanguay's dilemma: although comprehension and arithmetic remain problems throughout the NLDer's life, the weaknesses in the PIQ section are more preeminent in childhood. This VIQ>PIQ gap could close up somewhat as we grow older, and so it is harder to diagnose as such.

Fortunately, the newest versions of the Wechsler test, the WAIS-IV®, published in 2008,[30] and WISC-V®, published in 2014,[31] address and correct many of the problems of the older versions. So, should you be retested using the newer editions, your diagnosis is likely to be more objective than before. Of course, a precursor to any successful diagnosis is the perceived need that one should be diagnosed.

As revelatory as is the answer to Tanguay's dilemma, as helpful as are the new, improved Wechsler tests, and as innovative as is Palombo's research on subtypes, there still remain some very important unanswered questions. Whatever one might postulate are "core" symptoms, what proof is there that these must be "required," as opposed to saying that NLD is just one big conglomeration of random symptoms? Are any symptoms absolute, regardless of all the changes in life? Do any symptoms change or lessen over time, and if so, how and when? How many and which symptoms must there be, as a minimum, in order to diagnose NLD? Which "symptoms" may be just personality traits?

7: NLD symptoms change over time

One of my primary research questions was whether the actual symptoms of NLD change over time. What I found is that in most NLDers, some—but not all—of the symptoms can be overcome, compensated for, or reduced over time.

In the survey, subjects were asked to rate how well or poorly they did in various areas and skills—*academic*, *"executive functioning,"* *memory, social,* and *emotional*, such as understanding social cues, and *physical* skills—over time, at ages 6, 10, 14, 18, 22, 26, and 30. The ratings options were "poor," "fair," "good," and "very good."

There were some definite limitations to this otherwise ideal cross-sectional yet longitudinal study. Though more than 125 people responded to the survey, only about 40 completed all of this section. Only these completed surveys were left in the sample for the purpose of calculating the data. So the biggest limitation to this study, obviously, was the small sample size, which also dwindled with each age interval (there were only three people who were old enough to report on the skills at age 30).

The next limitation of the study was that these replies do not represent all of those with NLD, just those who not only found my website, but were motivated enough to take and complete the survey. Also, there was the issue of subjectivity—not only could anyone enter whatever they wanted, with no way for me to check the validity of their answers, but their ratings of the different skills and abilities were subject to their mood, their degree of fatigue, etc. at the time they took the survey. Adding to the issue of validity was that there was no way to know if the person taking the survey actually had NLD, and was in the target age range.

But even with all the ways the validity of my study could be challenged, one could still infer, by reading answers to the open-ended questions, that not only were the NLDers themselves taking the survey, but they were being perfectly candid and as objective as possible.

In the area of *academics*, math skills were quite varied, with some reporting always good, some always bad, and some good until they got to algebra. This finding is in noted contrast to previous literature about NLD, which states unequivocally that poor math skills are a hallmark of those with NLD. (For example, I aced math all the way through calculus III, so how could I possibly be classified as one of Rourke's "Group A" kids?)

Word skills were reported consistently as "very good," and with one exception, no one reported being "poor" or "fair." This trait seems to be absolute, that is, not changing over time. However, in reading comprehension, the average stays at "good" to age 14, drops, then picks up again at age 26. This may be a reflection either of schools not really preparing us (or our peers) for the typical college workload, slow development of the orbitofrontal cortex (the front of the brain responsible for focus), or there may be some other explanation.

In terms of *executive functioning* skills, for the ability to adapt easily to new situations, the results stay at "poor" to "fair" throughout the age span, until age 30, when they increase to "good," thus this is not absolute. The ability to improvise or ad-lib is absolute, at "fair," while both the ability to prioritize tasks and to multitask improve, with those ages 6–18 reporting "poor," and older respondents "fair."

All of the respondents reported being "poor" at managing time until around age 18, when they reported improving to "fair." Not one subject reported being "very good" at time management. The average ability to manage money was scattered, with the average "fair," but no trend over time.

These data show that not all "executive functioning" skills are created equal, nor are they all learned at the same time, save for three: prioritizing, managing time, and multitasking. As will be discussed in Chapter Seven, these three tasks are controlled by the same specific part of the brain, the dorsolateral prefrontal cortex. (From recent neurological research, we know that this part of the brain usually does not develop fully until after high-school age.)

In the area of *memory*, short-term attention is "poor" until age 22, then "good" to "very good" through age 26, while long-term attention is "fair" from ages 6 to 18, then "good" from 22 to 28 (with one reported "fair" at age 30). Aural rote memory average is consistently "good" throughout the age span, with the majority reporting "very good" balanced by a few "fairs" and "poors," and visual rote memory is consistently "good" throughout. Episodic memory, or remembering what happening in the past (such as where you were when some event happened) averages "good" throughout, with scattered responses, and the majority showing "very good" until age 22. In terms of remembering to do routine things, the results were consistently "fair."

In the area of *social-emotional* skills, the ability to deceive or to lie convincingly is "poor" from 6 to 14, then "fair." This may not sound like a desirable trait to have, unless you really think about what it would mean to always need to tell the whole truth and need to have people tell you the truth. (If you haven't considered the implications, consider watching the Jim Carrey movie *Liar, Liar* sometime.)

The ability to trust others is "good" at age 6, then stays at "fair" until age 30, while the ability to know when to trust others is consistently "fair" to "poor" at all age intervals. These data show that while we actually are able to trust others, we may not want to, because we may believe that others are untrustworthy. The ability to trust oneself is "poor to fair" from 6 to 18, "fair" at ages 22–26, and "good" at age 30, again showing improvement over time.

Self-esteem was reported as "fair/good" at age 6, "fair" at age 10, "poor/fair" at ages 14–22, and "fair" at ages 26–30, suggesting a dip in the adolescent years. Holding authority figures in esteem based on their title or rank alone was "fair/good" at ages 6–18, "fair" at ages 22–26, and "fair/good" at age 30.

The ability to listen to others and understand what they are talking about is "fair" at age 6, then "good" right until age 30. The ability to listen to others with an open mind averages "fair" for 6–18, then "good" from 22 to 30, though responses are scattered at all age intervals. Being able to perceive when others are listening to you is consistently "poor/fair" and is absolute.

The ability to show empathy when appropriate is "good" at age 6, "fair" at ages 10–18, "good" at ages 22–26, and "very good" at age 30, suggesting that we do improve with age, while the ability to assess the intensity of others' emotions is consistently "fair" throughout.

Being able to communicate one's feelings clearly is "poor/fair" from ages 5 to 10, "fair" at ages 14–22, and "good" at ages 26–30, showing steady improvement over time, but the ability to discern the way someone is feeling by the way they are talking (volume, intonation, facial expression, etc.) is consistently "fair" throughout.

In terms of "metacognition" (the ability to infer and understand others' motives), the value was absolute at "fair."

Physical traits vary. The ability to play a musical instrument averages "poor/fair" at ages 6–10, "fair" at ages 14–26, and is "good" at 30, the implication being that those who stick with it can become proficient musicians.

The ability to stand or sit still (as opposed to being fidgety) is consistently "fair" throughout the age span. Likewise, the ability to run or walk in a straight line is consistently "poor/fair" throughout, with no improvement over time. Handwriting (speed and legibility) is "poor" at ages 6–10, "poor/fair" at ages 14–22, improving only to "fair" at ages 26–30. And as for the ability to find one's way around in space, it is "fair" throughout the lifespan, with very scattered results.

What do all these data mean? What can we make of these findings?

The young adults interviewed and surveyed for this book have several traits in common. On average, they have a very good to excellent vocabulary, below-average motor skills (both gross and fine), as evidenced by their sloppy handwriting and, often, by their being fidgety—constantly moving into different positions or tapping their hands or fingers, or crossing and re-crossing their arms or legs.

One surprise was that contrary to findings in the previously existing NLD literature, only the women—not the entire sample— have poor math skills. High school math seems to be the great leveler, as the rating averages declined over time for both genders, but once respondents get to college, the men in the sample excelled in math, while the women did not improve.

Most had poor spatial skills (though one respondent said that his spatial skills are "excellent"), and in the early grades at least, many did poorly in spite of high effort, which belies their high intelligence.

Essentially every trait that has to do with understanding and communicating our *own* emotions and motives improves over time. But when it comes to understanding the emotions and motives of *other people*, those traits remain "fair" across the age span.

8: Not all symptoms are, in fact, symptoms

As the survey analysis shows, there are different rates of development for different symptoms of NLD. The traits that were ranked as "poor" to "fair" across the timespan given should be seen as core liabilities, just as those that are consistently "good" or "very good" should be seen as core assets. That there are some traits that improve steadily over time could indicate that they start out as core liabilities and are more apt to be "cured" one way or another over time, or that their improvement is just part of the natural development of NLD, or that the improvement is not really indicative of NLD development, but human development—it's not clear.

Perhaps the most interesting of all was that some of the traits— namely: reading comprehension, self-esteem, holding authority figures in esteem based on rank, ability to show empathy, and ability to trust others—started out good enough, then got worse over the course of the K-12 school experience, then got better starting at age 18. From this, we might conclude that these are mainly, if not exclusively, driven by the context and culture of the school environment. So, not all traits of NLD develop at the same rate; some absolute traits are assets, not symptoms; not all symptoms are due to deficits; and many of what previous researchers thought were absolute symptoms may be context specific.

As Tanguay[32] notes, the list of NLD symptoms may be confusing, as not all of us have all the symptoms, and not all have a particular subset of symptoms in the same combination and degree. Additionally, by the time we reach our teens, we are likely to have learned to use other strengths to compensate for some of the disabilities.

Is it any wonder that there is so much confusion about how to define and diagnose NLD? To the parents and teachers who deal with NLDers every day it may seem hopelessly frustrating. If after reading this far and answering the questions in Chapter One, you think you have NLD, you very well might. What does this mean? What is going on inside your brain? We will take a look in the next chapter.

Part II
The NLD Brain

Chapter Four

Understanding Your NLD Brain

It was so important to me to have evidence that I was not "making up" all these difficulties. Learning about the neurological basis of NLD gave me some solid scientific evidence to show my father, who thought that I was just spoiled and was "acting like a fool" to get out of things he thought I should be doing.

Because NLD may seem difficult to comprehend with respect to symptoms and diagnostic criteria, the most straightforward way to understand it logically is neurologically. So in this chapter and the next few, which will be technical and research-based, we are going to look at your brain, at some of the most common symptoms of NLD, and at which parts of the brain might be responsible for causing these symptoms.

As previously mentioned, every learning disability is based on some sort of neurological impairment. On the most basic level, NLD is the result of an imperfection of the structure of certain neurons in the brain. Psychologists consider it simply a disorder of cerebral white matter; white matter being "myelinated axons in the central nervous system."[33] But let's first look at what your brain does, what a neuron is, and how this relates to NLD.

Your brain is, effectively, a three-pound hunk of meat, shaped like a walnut and with the consistency of butter, which acts as a super-computer that controls the rest of your body, first via the spinal column, then via connected nerves. Like many other body organs, the brain is made up of proteins and fat and a few other chemicals—in this case, mostly omega-3 and omega-6 fatty acids, potassium, and sugars—and is part of the central nervous system, and therefore depends on the regulation of blood flow. This explains why holding your breath long enough gets you slightly dizzy—you're cutting off the oxygen to the blood that flows through your brain.

Looking at your brain as "a walnut," each half of the "walnut" is called a hemisphere. The two hemispheres are connected by a strip of membranous tissue called the corpus callosum, which is approximately as thin as the membranous tissue inside your nose that separates one nostril from the other. Through this tissue, each hemisphere can "communicate" with the other. With a few exceptions, the right hemisphere of the brain controls the left side of your body, and the left hemisphere controls the right side.

There is a great deal of plasticity to your brain, meaning that not only does the brain grow as your body grows and changes from birth to the end of puberty, it also grows as a result of learning new things.

The brain has three "layers:" the brain stem, the limbic system, and the neocortex. These are also often called the "reptilian brain," "mammalian brain," and "human brain" respectively, corresponding to the evolutionary divisions of the brain's development. Why?

The brain stem is similar to the entirety of the brain of modern reptiles. Therefore, the "reptilian brain" is about 500 million years old in terms of evolution. It is mainly responsible for regulating blood flow between the circulatory system and the central nervous system, for basic unconscious processes such as heartbeat, blood pressure, breathing, and automatic reflexes. Another main part of the reptilian brain is the cerebellum (Latin for "little brain"), which is responsible for coordination, controlled movement, and procedural memory, or knowing how to do something.

The limbic system—named the "mammalian brain" because it first emerged in mammals—is the center of your emotions, urges, and desires. There are several parts to the limbic system. The thalamus is the "middle man" for emotions, assigning each emotional function to a different part of the limbic system. The hypothalamus is mainly responsible for registering sexual drive, but if it malfunctions, it can be the source of many addiction-related problems. The pituitary gland regulates your physical growth. The amygdala stores unconscious traumatic memories and instinctually registers fear. The hippocampus is responsible for long-term memory related to finding your way around. The putamen is responsible for procedural memory, such as knowing how to tie shoes, and the caudate nucleus is responsible for many instincts and intuition.[34]

The neocortex has four main sections, called "lobes:" the occipital lobe at the back of your brain, which is mostly responsible for visual information; the temporal lobe, near your ears, responsible for auditory information and language; the parietal lobe, at the top of your brain, responsible for motor skills and sensory information; and the frontal lobe, at the front of your brain, which does the actual "thinking."

> *You may have all the book knowledge, but unless you have NLD you just don't get it completely. My brain works very, very hard just to appear "normal."*

Structure of a neuron, myelin, and "white matter"

The brain contains approximately 100 billion neurons, but amazingly enough, these nerve cells comprise only 10 percent of the total number of cells in the brain. The vast majority of other cells are glial cells, which hold the neurons together, and vascular cells, which form tissues for blood circulation.

A neuron is a nerve cell that is shaped approximately like an inverted tree. The cell nucleus is located next to the "branches," called dendrites, which receive electrical impulses from other neurons. These electrical impulses travel through the long, flexible "trunk" called the axon, and eventually get released through the "roots" to be received by other neurons. In most cases, the axon "trunk" has a "bark" on it called myelin, but there are certain parts along the axon "trunk" where the myelin "bark" is stripped off, and these exposed parts are called the nodes of Ranvier.

In general, your nervous system is "fed" by proteins called nerve growth factors, one of which, brain-derived neurotrophic factor (BDNF), is responsible for the production of myelin.[35] The purpose of myelin is to increase the rate of processing information "spiking" along the nodes of Ranvier, and thus to act as a kind of catalyst in propagating action potentials from one end of an axon to another.[36]

The fact that BDNF causes myelin production may seem insignificant at first, but read on. A general rule of neuroscience, called "Hebb's Law"—named after Donald O. Hebb, who proposed it in 1949—is that "neurons that fire together wire together," meaning that when neurons fire at the same time, chemical changes occur in each that link them together more strongly. BDNF makes this happen. Moreover, BDNF regulates the beginning and end points of the critical period—the period between birth and two years old in neurotypical humans, when one must receive a minimum level of visual input to prevent blindness that was not genetically pre-ordained—and tells the nucleus basalis what to pay attention to during this time.[37]

So what does all this have to do with NLD?

Left versus right

As you have just read, the level and timing of the first increase in myelin is a definitive factor of NLD. But what of a decrease? Many experts, starting with Rourke,[38] posited that demyelination (reduction of myelin) exacerbates the symptoms of NLD when it occurs in the right hemisphere of the brain more than in the left hemisphere. As you just read, the two hemispheres are connected by the corpus callosum, through which each hemisphere can "communicate" with the other.

When talking about NLD, psychologists dwell mainly on the "problem" of the right hemisphere—occasionally in lieu of other possibilities—because it is generally accepted psychological theory that the left hemisphere focuses on the "details," such as math and word skills, deductive and inductive logic, spoken language, scientific skills, and others; while the right hemisphere focuses on the "big picture:" insight, art appreciation, music appreciation, 3-D forms, creativity, and imagination, among others. The natural inclination is for psychologists to lateralize symptoms—that is, to say it must be due to a deficiency in one hemisphere or the other. For many NLD symptoms, this actually is not wrong.

NLD in 3-D?

But there is more to the brain than just the left hemisphere versus the right. Even Rourke had to admit this. He postulated that white matter is not just one big homogeneous glob of myelin; instead there are three types of neurons that, when myelinated, comprise white matter. The first set is Association (Back ↔ Front) Fibers, which interconnect different lobes within the same hemisphere, and on which the left hemisphere is more "dependent." The next set are Projection (Down ↔ Up) Fibers, which act as the basic input–output system between the cerebral hemispheres and the diencephalons, the front part of the limbic system. Commissural (Right ↔ Left) Fibers go through the corpus callosum, on which the right hemisphere is more "dependent," and therefore if damaged, would be the prime cause of NLD.[39]

Still, this misses the point. NLD is not limited in scope simply to a matter of being a "right hemisphere disorder," nor was it ever intended as such by Johnson and Myklebust, who said that it was merely the hemisphere that controls the non-dominant side of the body—not just the right hemisphere—that was at fault. When I first proposed the topic of NLD as my senior thesis to Dr. David Stevens, my advisor at Clark University, he asked me, "How can it possibly be that NLD is just a right hemisphere disorder? It sounds as if all there is to it is just a bunch of holes punched out of the right hemisphere of the brain, and all of a sudden, ta-da! You have NLD! That just doesn't make sense."[40] I had to admit, he was right. So I threw out the "conventional wisdom" and started again by approaching NLD on a symptom-by-symptom basis. The next chapters will describe what I found.

Chapter Five

Sensory Sensitivities and the NLD Brain

Some of us NLDers lack awareness of the importance of basic life skills, such as how to dress appropriately for school, work, or social events, or of commonly accepted rules of etiquette. We may not even understand the importance of the fundamentals of hygiene, such as knowing enough to shower, wear deodorant, or brush our teeth regularly. If simply not remembering to do these is the case, then this is caused by a lack of "communication" between the putamen and the cerebellum. But much of the time, these instances of "forgetting" to attend to hygiene are actually connected to sensory sensitivity issues:

> *When I first went away from home (to a summer program), I didn't brush my teeth for the entire summer. I know, I know, now it sounds gross, but at the time, I just could not stand the taste of the tap water in the bathroom. And I didn't know what else to do. Now that I'm older, I would know enough to bring some bottled water into the bathroom with me, but at the time that just would not have occurred to me.*

> *This is kind of embarrassing to think back on now, but when I first got my period, I couldn't deal with it. My mother tried to give me all sorts of sanitary napkins, belts, stick-on pads, everything—but everything felt terribly itchy to me and it chafed. All I wanted to do was to sit at home in the bathtub for the whole four days every month.*

From where do these sensory sensitivity issues come?

According to neuroplasticity expert Michael Merzenich, who has researched the root causes of autism, it has to do with frontloading of BDNF.

According to Merzenich, those with autism are born with a genetic tendency to be much more sensitive to BDNF in the critical period, the first two years of life, than are their neurotypical peers. If, in those first two years, the autistic child's brain is overexcited, then there is a massive, premature release of BDNF, causing the neurons to grow myelin much faster than usual, neural connections to be made indiscriminately, and the critical period to be shut down early.

If the overexcitement is auditory, the child will develop a hypersensitivity to certain sounds; if the overexcitement is visual, the child will develop a hypersensitivity to certain lights; if the overexcitement is tactile, the child will develop a hypersensitivity to certain textures. But the fact that neurons are so interconnected means that whenever they are overstimulated, it is as though their whole brain is being overstimulated all at once.[41]

According to Merzenich, the real reason autism (and perhaps all Autism Spectrum Disorders) is so much more prevalent now than it used to be—once increased diagnosis is factored in—is that "infants are reared in continuously more noisy environments. There is always a din…every time you have a pulse, you are excited [sic] everything in the auditory cortex—every neuron."[42]

Merzenich is arguing that, as technology advances, and we are raised around more white noise (multiple sound frequencies at once, often rapidly pulsing, which are very stimulating), and more strobe lights (multiple light frequencies at once, often rapidly pulsing, which are very stimulating), the more cases of the critical period shutting down early because this bombardment of input is too much too soon, leading to more diagnoses of developmental disabilities later on. That is probably the best argument for the rise of autism I have ever heard.

But this isn't just about autism. Recall Whitney's three-fold explanation for the rise of NLD mentioned earlier: genetics, environmental toxins, and shifts in behavioral patterns and expectations. Viewed through the lens of Merzenich's theory, Whitney has won the trifecta in explaining NLD among developmental disabilities on the basis of sensory sensitivity alone.

So, how do sensory sensitivities work?

In general, a sensory receptor is a sensory nerve ending of a neuron, wherein the cell nucleus is located either among or in place of the dendrites, and registers a response to a stimulus, either internally or externally. Upon receiving the stimulus, the sensory neuron sends a signal directly to the motor cortex to identify what just happened, as well as to the amygdala to gut-check whether what just happened was OK or not. If not, we have a problem.

NLD and stress

I am SO stressed out so much of the time. I wish my family, friends, teachers, and doctors know how hard it is to live with NLD. Maybe if they understood more, they would stop making me feel worse.

Many NLDers feel stressed much of the time. Here's how stress works. As soon as the amygdala senses danger, from whatever source, it conveys to the hypothalamus a basic message: "Danger, danger, do something!"

At that point, the hypothalamus sends a signal to the adrenal glands, located at the top of the kidneys, to release glucocorticoids, or stress hormones. The first stress hormone released is adrenaline (also called epinephrine), which makes your heart beat faster, your blood pressure rise, your body sweat, etc. The second, perhaps more dangerous stress hormone, is cortisol.[43]

And while acute stress may act as a temporary pain relief, chronic stress does the reverse, as a constant bombardment of glucocorticoids frequently can lead to high blood pressure, heart attack, stroke, and weakened immune system function.[44] Also, chronic stress can even destroy the BDNF that makes your brain work, and when the BDNF is attacked, so is the ability to learn effectively.[45]

So what is the solution? Simple: exercise. Countless studies show that exercise improves your heart, lowers your blood pressure, and strengthens your immune system. Exercise actually can improve your brain function, reduce anger,[46] help you to learn better, and even improve your grades![47]

Microbiologist John Medina explains how exercise helps you get rid of stress:

> When you exercise, you increase blood flow across the tissues of your body. This is because exercise stimulates the blood vessels to create a powerful, flow-regulating molecule called nitric oxide. As the flow improves, the body makes new blood vessels... This allows more access to the bloodstream's goods and services, which include food

distribution and waste disposal. The more you exercise, the more tissues you can feed and the more toxic waste you can remove. This happens all over the body. That's why exercise improves the performance of most human functions... The same happens in the human brain.[48]

As for how much exercise, the latest research shows that we need at least 150 minutes of moderate exercise each week, or 30 minutes/day for five days each week. What type of exercise you choose is entirely up to you, but if you need some suggestions, here are a few from our interviewees and survey respondents.

Walking: Whether taking a stroll around the neighborhood, doing laps around a track with your iPod cranked up, or walking your dog, this is one of the most therapeutic, gentle-to-your-body, tried-and-true forms of exercise. The speed, direction, and company—whether human or animal—are all up to you.

Dancing: You can take classes in trendy dances like NIA or Zumba, or go old school and just blast your favorite CD and dance freestyle at home. There's something for everyone. However, use caution about going into clubs, especially if you have sensory sensitivity issues pertaining to light or sound.

Biking: Riding your bike on the road or on a trail, or even riding a stationary bike, is a good way to use all your major muscle groups.

Swimming: Doing laps, diving, playing water games, or working out in the water can be really fun, and helps you work off stress.

Obviously, there are many different forms of exercise from which to choose, including both team sports and individual pursuits. But whatever the activity and intensity level, from shooting hoops to shooting pool to skeet shooting, the goal is to find an enjoyable way to move around. With good exercise, your brain will function optimally, to help you function well as you go about your daily life.

Blood, sweat, and tears

How does this relate to sensory sensitivities? Every single part of your body depends on sensory receptors—especially the inside. When exercise is stimulating your blood vessels, and they're doing their thing making nitric oxide, all of this flow of blood is regulated by baroreceptors, which are sensory neurons in the blood. They sense the blood pressure and relay the information to the brain, which then relays the information back to the heart, so that a proper blood pressure can be maintained.

Also, have you ever noticed that you sweat when you exercise? You can thank your osmoreceptors for that. Osmoreceptors are sensory receptors primarily found in the hypothalamus. They regulate osmotic pressure and contribute to fluid balance in the body, which means they maintain a healthy water/salt ratio in your body, and let you know when you are or are not thirsty.

In addition to applications to exercise, baroreceptors and osmoreceptors are responsible for all circulatory and water duct regulation, respectively. That's why it follows that baroreceptors respond to every part of your body that relies on the circulatory system.

> I also had an eating disorder in high school, so that accounted for not being able to tell if I was hungry or not.

There is one more set of internal sensory receptors worth mentioning: proprioceptors.

Coordination

Proprioceptors, located in your inner ear, relay information directly to the cerebellum, to give you a sense of where you are relative to the space around your body. The brain integrates information from proprioception and from the vestibular system into its overall sense of body position, movement, equilibrium, and acceleration, and provides a sense of gravity. Basically, it's what keeps you from being a klutz, and for the most part, prevents you from getting dizzy. Most of the time, this shouldn't be a problem, but since NLDers are known for motor deficits, this occasionally can prove problematic.

> I absolutely LOVE going to the library, and if it were up to me, I'd go to a new one every week. But the old, historic library in my hometown has stairs that terrify me. It's bad enough that you have to walk upstairs to get to the main floor, but I simply cannot STAND going up to the stacks. The stairs up there are so narrow, and the open railings on the walkway between the two sides are so low! Even though I'm a grown man, if no one else is around, sometimes I'll crawl across the walkway, if I absolutely have to get across.

Lost in space

Proprioception problems augmented with vision problems can cause even more problems. For example, a lesion on the right side of the brain in the region of the parietal lobe closest to the occipital lobe, which corresponds both to being able to see two things at the same time and to spatial awareness (for example, the ability to mentally rotate objects in space) will cause someone to be unable to find their way around in space. This inferior spatial orientation is a very common problem among NLDers and usually at least one of their parents as well.

> *While playing Little League baseball in the fifth grade, I hit a single. When I was about halfway to first base, I saw the second baseman pick up the ball. I thought there was no chance I could make it to first base, so I just ran off the field. My teammates were mad, and told me I could've easily made it. To me the distance looked enormous, even insurmountable.*

Moreover, if the right side of the hippocampus, responsible for "big picture" memory, is damaged, the problem could also extend to getting lost in the most familiar settings.[49] This would account for the phenomenon of not being able to figure out how to drive from your house to the nearest highway, even though all the streets and landmarks in between are perfectly familiar.

> *At this point in my life, the most frustrating thing is my spatial/ directional difficulties, because I want very much to adapt and drive well to any location I want, but the fact is that with a new place it takes me maybe a couple of practice tries—or more.*

It would not be surprising to find an elementary school child with NLD emulating Hansel and Gretel by placing physical markers along the path to help find the way back to school from recess. Of course, this is contingent on the notion that he or she would think to do such a thing in the first place.

> *Once, during kindergarten recess, I followed a butterfly into the woods, because I wanted to see where he lived. I didn't hear the bell, or the teacher calling me back. No one could find me, and all the teachers and staff, even the principal, had to go out looking for me. After that, the*

school didn't know what to do with me, so for first grade, they put me into SPED.

Feeling the pain

When most people hear the term "sensory sensitivities," they think of the "big five,"—touch, taste, smell, sight, and sound—which collectively are known as exteroception. Primary among these are tactile nociceptors. Nociceptors are sensory neurons that respond to potentially damaging stimuli by sending signals to the spinal cord and brain. The sensation of pain is registered in the periaqueductal grey area of the midbrain. This process, called nociception, causes the perception of physical pain.

I HATE labels in my shirts! They scratch my skin and feel awful. I would wait until I got to school, then go into the girls' room and turn my shirts inside out. A lot of kids would make fun of me and that was harsh, but it was better than feeling like my skin was being torn to ribbons daily.

Nociceptors do occur surrounding internal organs, and hence can cause stomachaches, headaches, etc. But the skin gets most of the "hype," as it deals with such a wide range of tactile sensations: itchiness, sliminess, smoothness, bumpiness, etc., and can cause a general feeling of unpleasantness. In addition to simply sensing texture, there are different subcategories of tactile nociceptors. Hydroreceptors, for example, are responsible for sensing how wet or dry you are, and if you have a low threshold of pain, a shower or rain can feel like thousands of pencil points poking your skin.

Mechanoreceptors respond to excess pressure to the skin, mechanical deformation of the skin, and incisions that break the skin surface. Hypersensitivity here might manifest as the need to not be hugged or kissed. Being sensitive in this way might seem to others as if you're rejecting their affection, but that's not the cause. Also, the next time you feel the need to crack your knuckles or your neck, you can tell that's because your mechanoreceptors need a break.

I sleep with a weighted blanket. I wish I'd known about those when I was little. I used to be sleeping with the windows open and fans on in the summer and have six blankets on top of me.

Thermoreceptors are activated by noxious heat or cold at various temperatures. There are specific nociceptor transducers that are responsible for how and if the specific nerve ending responds to the thermal stimulus. Because thermoreceptors respond to both heat and cold, there are certain types responsible for cold threshold, some responsible for heat threshold, and some that respond to the sudden shift from heat to cold or vice versa.

If you can believe your own eyes and ears

But exteroception is not limited to your skin—far from it! Have you ever found that you couldn't stand how loud someone was blasting their music, and gone over to them to request very nicely that they turn it down, only to have them "point out" that it was at a "reasonable volume," and really, you were the only one complaining? Aural nociceptors are at the heart of this dispute. Located in the hairs in your ear, and occupying much of the same neural network as proprioceptors—running the length from the inner ear to the brain, but ending in the temporal lobe instead of the cerebellum—aural nociceptors respond to bass, treble, midrange, and overall volume of a given noise.

Likewise, electromagnetic radiation (visual) receptors respond to the full spectrum of light. Infrared receptors respond to infrared radiation, ultraviolet receptors respond to ultraviolet radiation, and photoreceptors respond to visible light. Photoreceptors are located in the retina, both in the rods, which are responsible for distinguishing between brightness and darkness, and cones, responsible for color distinction. For those who are photosensitive, bright lights, flashing lights, strobe lights, flickering lights—such as candlelight, faulty fluorescent bulbs, or even dappling sunlight through leaves—can cause physical problems, such as seizures, nausea, or migraine headaches.

Chemical reactions

Chemoceptors are found in the nose and tongue. Smell chemo-receptors are receptor neurons in the olfactory system. Olfaction, or smell, involves the ability to detect chemicals in the gaseous state, specifically, odorants and pheromones, found in the nasal cavity and that affect the oxygen level in the brain.

Taste chemoreceptors are located on taste buds in the gustatory system. Various chemical compounds come into contact with chemoreceptors in the mouth, such as taste buds on your tongue, and trigger responses: either an appetitive response for nutrients— you are hungry—or a defensive response against toxins—it tastes yucky—depending on which receptors fire. But, for the tongue, it doesn't stop with chemoreceptors, but also involves nociceptors, since the tongue has plenty of texture "issues" of its own.

> *I wish they had known (I wish my father could get this pounded into his thick head now, actually, as he still thinks I'm making it up) that I wasn't having meltdowns on purpose, and that I really "couldn't" eat the food on my plate due to sensory sensitivities.*

It's worth mentioning that just as one person may be hypersensitive to a given stimulus, another person may be equally "off" by being hyposensitive—perhaps even to the point of being completely numb to that stimulus. And each of us has our own combination of "highs" and "lows," which may be subject to change in severity over time.

However we may react to any given sensory input, we all seem to "know" how a given sensory input "should" make us feel, based on how sensory input has crept into our language.[50] If you're tired and aching, you say you had a "hard day" at work. You might call your lover "honey" or "sweetheart," but you'd probably be repulsed by love songs that are too "syrupy" or "saccharine." If you think someone is lying to you, you might say their story is "fishy," or maybe you "smell a rat," or it could "stink to high heaven." The ability to understand sensory input idioms ultimately leads to improved social understanding, as you'll see in the next chapter.

Chapter Six

Social Cues and the NLD Brain

Do you have trouble understanding what people actually mean when they are talking to you? Or, worse, when they say one thing and seem to mean another—for example, when they are being sarcastic or speaking metaphorically? Do you miss nuances in conversation? If so, you are not alone. Another common symptom of NLD is a lack of understanding social cues—what people mean when they don't say what they mean—or when they use body language or facial expressions to show how they feel. Not only are these nonverbal communications difficult or impossible for us to interpret, often we also do not know how to respond. An example from one of the first interviews for this book illustrates this point:

> *[We met] in a small coffee shop/bookstore…we sat down in two big leather chairs in the lounge, and began. I started out the interview with the question, "How are you doing?" and he asked, "What do you mean, 'how am I doing?'" I then stopped the tape recorder, and rewound it. He then started to question me on why I was asking, and what this interview was all about [even though I had previously explained it to him on the phone]. I proceeded to tell him that this was a senior thesis I was doing for my psychology major, and that I had NLD, and that a big part of my study was collecting other first-hand accounts. Only then did he say that he understood, and I said, "OK, when I ask you, 'How are you doing' this time, I mean it as an icebreaker." He then said, "OK." I turned on the tape recorder to record over the "false start" and we began again.*

The lack of ability to pick up on social cues is a hallmark of NLD. One explanation might be found in a trend in neuroscientific research: the study of mirror neurons, first discovered in 1995 by Iaccomo Rizzolatti and Vittorio Gallese, researchers at the University of Parma, who worked with macaque monkeys. While measuring neural activities of these monkeys who were eating, the researchers discovered that the areas of the monkeys' brains that were active when they reached for a peanut also were active in the monkeys' brains when they watched the human researchers reach for a peanut. It appeared that the monkeys' brains didn't register the difference between when they themselves reached for the peanut and when they saw someone else do it!

How does this story relate to NLD?

Suppose that this (at least partial) inability to tell the difference between your own actions and someone else's actions could apply to humans. What might this mean? Rizzolatti and Gallese's work generated much interest among other neurologists. In 2005, Marco Iacoboni and his team of fellow researchers at UCLA published a study that said that the neurons in the human anterior cingulate cortex (located at the back and bottom of the frontal lobe, adjacent to the outermost part of the limbic system), which fire when one experiences pain (such as when one is being poked with a needle) also fire when someone *else* is in pain.[51]

Dozens of subsequent studies prove that for humans, information is received in certain parts of the brain when they observe someone else do something that mirrors the information they themselves would get from doing the same thing. Visual information is received in the occipital lobe, auditory in the temporal lobe, and motor and sensory in the parietal lobe. And when this information is sent to the limbic system, they connect the actions with the usual associated emotions.

As an automatic reflex, they laugh when others laugh, cry when others cry, etc. And when all of this emotional information gets sent to the orbitofrontal cortex, neurotypical people sort it all out, and understand what the feelings mean and why others are feeling the way they are. So they are, in essence, first being empathic, and then, perhaps, even understanding of others' motives. But this applies only to the neurotypical human.

We NLDers can laugh when others laugh, and wince when we see someone get slammed, just like everyone else, but it is the ability, or lack thereof, to understand emotions—not only our own but others'—that's the problem.

And it's not just a symptom of NLD; it also tends to be true of those disorders in the "Autism Spectrum": autism, High Functioning Autism, pervasive developmental disorder (PDD), and Asperger's Syndrome. This lack occurring in these disorders is caused primarily by a deficit of neural communication in the mirror neuron system, specifically in the connection between the right orbitofrontal cortex and the amygdala.[52] It causes both a reduced capacity for empathy and for dyssemia, which is difficulty understanding and using nonverbal "signs," such as reading facial expressions and interpreting tone of voice.[53]

Except…there may be a bit of a problem.

Too much monkey business?

The problem with the mirror neuron theory is that the whole "monkey see, monkey do" premise may be just that—some to most of the means of imitation may not translate from monkey to human, and vice versa, according to the latest research on mirror neurons. In fact, even the researchers at Parma weren't sure exactly *why* the macaques were reaching for the peanuts when they did. Was it strict behaviorist training? Maybe the monkeys were making sure the amount of food they got always matched or exceeded the researchers' so they were never going to take the monkeys' stash? Maybe the monkeys were making sure the food was evenly distributed as a counting mechanism?

In his 2014 book, *The Myth of Mirror Neurons*,[54] Gregory Hickok points out the flaws in the mirror neuron theory, from what can go wrong with visual input to motor output to understanding cause and effect, as well as pointing out the (mostly post hoc) fallacies in the leap from copying movements to copying emotions.

To be fair, barring any major impediment to the visual input → motor output → understanding chain, babies are apt to try out virtually any form of imitation they can, starting with motoric, as evidenced by numerous cases—scientific and lay—of a baby sticking out his/her tongue after looking at an adult stick out his/hers (to cite one classic example). So maybe the mirror neuron theory applies in that sense.

But as children grow older, they figure out which actions can be performed when and where, and then from that, as they learn the consequences of those actions, they start to understand cause and effect. Eventually, this cause and effect also includes conditionals and qualifiers that necessitate sorting out how to behave in different social settings and situations like, "I can do X only when I'm alone," or, "…when I'm with Mom, but not when I'm with Dad," or, "… when I'm at school, but not when I'm at church," or, "…when I'm at this restaurant, but not at that restaurant," and so on.

And as we semi-consciously build up this huge, complex algorithm of *if-then* statements, and then have to factor in all the exceptions, and the exceptions to the exceptions, and the exceptions to the exceptions to the exceptions, it gives our brains a lot to think about and worry about, not to mention worrying about whether we're worrying too much, which can get quite cumbersome! How to explain all this?

The real deal on empathy

So far, we have one camp saying that mirror neurons are legit and responsible for all things empathic, and another camp saying this is all bogus. Who is right?

As it turns out, they both are correct, because there are, in fact, two different types of empathy: cognitive empathy and affective empathy. Cognitive empathy deals with understanding feelings on an impersonal level, whereas affective empathy has to do with actually feeling those feelings on a visceral level.

But because, as you read in Chapter Three, NLDers often may understand their own feelings, but not those of others, before we get to the "empathy" part, we have to understand the roots of each. These are, quite simply, the old "emotions versus logic" dichotomy— affection versus cognition.

Affection, in its truest sense, is an emotion felt on a visceral level that influences behavior. This comes from the amygdala, with some help from the thalamus, and other parts of the limbic system. Cognition has nothing to do with the limbic system, and everything to do with the neocortex.

As Dr. Kevin Dutton explains:

…it involves those areas of the brain, the prefrontal cortex and posterior parietal cortex (in particular the anterior paracingulate cortex, the temporal pole, and the superior temporal sulcus), principally implicated in our objective experience of cold empathy: in reasoning and rational thoughts.[55]

But in order for the affective and cognitive sides to "graduate" to affective and cognitive empathy, one has to understand that others might have feelings and thoughts similar to one's own. If done correctly, both systems will "talk" to each other to figure out that, "if I feel or think X under Y circumstances, then so should you." But, the results will again be different. Affective empathy, then, is feeling on a visceral level what others feel, and thus gives credence to the mirror neuron system, which is powered by the neurotransmitter oxytocin, which is passed through skin-to-skin contact.

For cognitive empathy, this means that understanding that if you follow the complex *if-then* algorithm discussed above of when and how to act in certain situations then so must others, with some modifications. This, then, is metacognition, or "theory of mind": the understanding that others' beliefs, intentions, and points of view might be different from yours, because their *if-then* algorithms might yield different results. And this ability, as well as the attempt to find a quick, logical solution to an emotion-laden problem, is governed by the temperoparietal junction (TPJ), which is powered by testosterone, which explains, in large part, why women and men handle emotional situations so differently from one another.[56]

If these two forms of empathy also involve an element of episodic memory, which is memory of where you were at a certain time, then they both "graduate" to sympathy. "Affective sympathy" occurs when you react viscerally to the thought of someone else feeling a certain way, since you remember feeling that way in the past. Likewise, cognitive sympathy is when you "feel for someone" because you "have been there before," and this happens because you remember running the "how-and-why-to-act" algorithm through your head, based either on your own or someone else's experience.

Therefore, what happens is that the mirror neuron system or TPJ, respectively, gets added information from the hippocampus, responsible for episodic memory, and from the ventromedial prefrontal cortex, which deals with coding perception, and the memory of how you felt at that time.

Whether or not people with autism truly lack "theory of mind," or they just lack a means of voicing what it is they feel (technically known as alexithymia), NLDers lack neither affective empathy nor cognitive empathy, nor, for the most part, affective and cognitive sympathy. Instead, we may have problems with these two systems communicating with each other. This often may result in situations such as when, if attending a funeral of someone not especially close, an NLDer might think, "you may be feeling grief, but what does that have to do with me?"

Additionally, the right orbitofrontal cortex's two next-door neighbors, the anterior cingulate cortex and the rostral cingulated zone, have a lot to do with the true nature of social skills, according to neurologist Louann Brizendine, M.D.[57] Brizendine describes the anterior cingulate cortex (ACC) as:

> the worry-wart, fear-of-punishment area, and center of sexual performance anxiety. It's smaller in men than in women. It weighs options, detects conflicts, motivates decisions. Testosterone decreases worries about punishment. The ACC is also the area for self-consciousness.[58]

There, it would seem that if this area is not working well in an NLDer, it might account for our being over trusting and for our naïveté.

Yet even more important is the rostral cingulate zone (RCZ), which Brizendine describes as:

> the brain's barometer for registering social approval or disapproval. This "I am accepted or not" area keeps humans from making the most fundamental social mistake: being too different from others. The RCZ is the brain center for processing social errors...[59]

Needless to say, if the "brain center for processing social errors" isn't working well, it can lead to some serious faux pas.

> *Well, I used to complain about things that, at inopportune times, like at a birthday party once, the cake was an ice cream cake, and I started complaining about that, and my mom had to say to me, "Quiet down, it's a birthday party." Well, you know, I'm more conscious of that now.*

So cognition, metacognition, and decision-making affect social understanding. But how do you know which decision to make? How do you know if a decision is "right" or "wrong"? And what, exactly, is "executive functioning" all about? Read on.

Chapter Seven

Executive Functioning and the NLD Brain

There are probably as many different explanations of what executive functioning is as there are experts. However, some of the most frequent executive functioning skill deficits thought to be associated with NLD are difficulties with: planning, prioritizing, organizing, sequencing, short-term attention, multitasking, retention, goal-setting, problem-solving, money management, and impulse control. Even reading this list may sound overwhelming to someone with NLD. To make it simpler, what executive functioning really boils down to is the extent to which the brain can figure out:

- what to attend to

- when to attend to it

- how much can be remembered at once

- how long any given piece of information should be retained

- how to retain it.

"But, wait!" you might say, "These are executive functioning areas that are associated with ADD *and* NLD?!" Yes, that's right—both have the same areas of difficulty. In fact, one interviewee answered the question "What does NLD mean to you?" as follows:

Well, usually when I have the different thought processes, it's something that's been going through inside my mind, rather than something I see on the outside [here he waves his hand, gesturing a dismissal], then, it's difficulty with academics. And possibly with organizational thought. I guess that's something I forgot.

Organizational difficulties, yeah, definitely.

Lack of planning skills

One section of the prefrontal cortex, the dorsolateral prefrontal cortex, is often dubbed "the central executive," hence the term "executive functioning" to describe its role in planning and prioritizing and sequencing thought and actions. Many people with NLD have difficulty with tasks that require planning, though they are quite capable of doing all the tasks in a plan once it is made.

> *When I was about seven or eight, my mom would come in and tell me, "You have to clean your room now." And I would say, "OK." But then I would look at the mess and just throw myself down on the bed and cry. All I knew is that the mess was too big, and I could never do it. I would get frustrated and my mom would get angry. I'm not sure if she ever read anything about how to help me, but she finally figured out a system that worked. She made me a chart that said: #1: Make the bed. #2: Put all the toys into the toy box. #3: Put all the dirty clothes into the clothes hamper. #4: Put the clean clothes into the drawers, etc. No one part of this was too hard for me to do, it was just that I could not figure out the steps on my own. We had not yet heard of "executive functioning" skills, and I didn't know I was deficient in them.*

The purpose of this brain function is to oversee how memory is operating: "Things are held 'in mind' here, and manipulated to form plans and concepts. This area also seems to choose to do one thing over another."[60] In other words, to prioritize.

These tasks are notoriously difficult for those with NLD. The process of setting up and actually conducting the initial interviews for this book illustrates the challenges in planning skills experienced by most of us with NLD. Listen to what happened:

> *When I arrived at 12:58 pm at the college library, I went straight to stack three, where she [the subject] told me she would meet me at 1:00 pm. I waited until 1:12 pm, and she still wasn't there. Then I went back into the main area of the library, asked a girl sitting on a couch, if she had seen who I was looking for, and she replied, "Oh, that's me!" So we had*

to start at 1:15 pm. This is so typical of two NLD individuals that we both laughed.

[We] met on the main floor of the library. I waited for him for about 20 minutes before he actually showed up. Since I wasn't sure he would remember the appointment, I had emailed him the day before. When I did not get an answer by about an hour before the interview, I called his dorm room and apparently woke him up. I apologized, and he complained, "Why did you have to wake me up now? It's not for an hour, is it?" But then, when he finally showed up, he grudgingly acknowledged that without my phone call, he would have slept right through the appointment. He was still wearing his pajamas, but with a trench coat over them. On his feet, he wore flip-flops. In February. When it was snowing outside. His hair was completely disheveled, and he apparently had chosen not to shave for about two weeks. Despite his fatigue, he was pleasant and funny and the interview proceeded smoothly, once we found a place to do it.

[For the third one] we had to look all over the library for a quiet space. I first asked the guy at the circulation desk if we could have the conference room I had used for the interview last week. He said no, so we looked all over the fourth floor for a place that was at least semi-private. Not only did it take us about 20 minutes to find a good place, but we both were getting incredibly lost. We finally started at about 11:45 am, for the interview that had been scheduled for 11:00 am. Again, I had to laugh at the predictably unpredictable scenario of two people with NLD trying to do an interview.

It is therefore reasonable to assume that the "central executive" section of the brain, responsible for deciding what to remember, is a likely candidate for being damaged in NLD. Yet once the brain has locked in on what it wants to remember, if NLDers lack the ability to "coordinate incoming information with information already in the system,"[61] is it really any surprise, then, that we are so resistant to virtually any change?

OK, I admit it. Looking back, it even seems kind of silly now. But when my parents took out the '80s-style track lighting in the living room to replace it with recessed lighting, I actually lay down on the floor and cried. I mean, the lights have been that way my whole life. I don't like things to change.

When my family travels on vacation, I have a hard time adjusting to sleeping in a hotel. Don't get me wrong—I really like going on vacation, but the bed is different, the smells and sounds are different, the food is different and that always takes some getting used to. After the first few days, it's not so bad. But I am always very happy to come home again.

It is incredibly difficult for me if they change the bell schedule in school for any reason—like an assembly or a teachers' meeting or something. I know where I am supposed to be at any given time on a particular day, but if they switch the schedule from an "A" day to a "B" day, I get very, very anxious.

Will/want/won't power

The entire history of behaviorist psychology—from Ivan Pavlov's drooling dogs to modern-day addiction studies—shows that we humans don't have as much free will as we'd like to think. Why is this? Blame it on dopamine. Dopamine, one of the most common neurotransmitters, is responsible for the "pleasure principle." You receive a sensory input that first gets the OK from the amygdala. Then the thalamus gives it the thumbs-up, which means that not only is this not bad, it's good enough to arouse your appetite for it. The thalamus then tells the nucleus accumbens, "Go for it!" The nucleus accumbens sends a flood of dopamine to the dorsolateral prefrontal cortex, saying, "I want it. I want it. I want it. Gimme, gimme, gimme!"

Most of the time, the dorsolateral prefrontal cortex succumbs. When it does so, the orbitofrontal cortex gets the message and files it under "good decision." But as the early behaviorists showed, dopamine doesn't just fire in the presence of a treat. It also fires in the anticipation of one. The anterior cingulate cortex comes in to act as a fact-checker.

If the thought of a perceived reward doesn't match the actuality of the payoff, the orbitofrontal cortex has to reclassify it as a "bad decision." When this happens, the insula becomes more "aware" of the "cons" of a perceived reward, and it fires dopamine to argue against what the nucleus accumbens is arguing for.[62]

Consider this: you are in a restaurant, you've just enjoyed a great meal, and now are contemplating ordering a dessert. You scroll through the options, and you decide that what you really want is their famous Triple-Layer Coconut Cake à la Mode. The internal dialogue between your nucleus accumbens (Nacc) and your insula (In) might go something like this:

Nacc: "Mmmm... dessert. You know, I think I'm hungry again."

In: "You can't possibly be hungry! You know as well as I do that Stomach just sent all of us here in Brain a bunch of leptin telling us that it's full."

Nacc: "Forget Stomach! Have you *seen* that cake?!"

In: "Yeah, and it must be 1,500 calories for one slice."

Nacc: "Oh, whatever! It looks sooooo delicious."

In: "Did you check out the price? Ten dollars for a piece of cake? You probably could get two whole supermarket brand cakes for that price."

Nacc: "Sure, but would they taste as good as this one? How often do I get to come to this restaurant, anyway? I'd pay 20 dollars just to have you shut up for once."

In: "You would, wouldn't you? Fine, go ahead, order the cake. But you'll regret it."

Nacc: "Thank you, I think I will."

End result: the dorsolateral prefrontal cortex weighs both sides, the nucleus accumbens wins, you order the cake, enjoy it, and maybe regret it when you get on the scale the next morning, at which point, the anterior cingulate cortex bolsters the case made by the insula.

If the nucleus accumbens keeps winning out again and again and again, eventually what ends up happening is that you become addicted to that stimulus—be it sugar, sex, gambling, drugs, alcohol, or any other means of having a stimulus mess with your head (as it were). Eventually, the logical dorsolateral prefrontal cortex may stop working the way it should, in the form of rationalizing bad behavior, and other neurotransmitters may step in to divert the stream of dopamine or shut it down altogether.

Alternately, if the insula is on overdrive, then you may just not care to even try anything new at all, and this apathy may be accompanied by engaging in endless "negative self-talk." Considering that the insula is the next-door neighbor to the language cortex (more about which you'll learn in the next chapter), this shouldn't come as a surprise. So the question is: how can the decision-making process be more rational, and less driven by dopamine impulses?

Impulse control and emotional maturity

Another common symptom of those with NLD is poor impulse control. In addition to being responsible for filing decisions made by the dorsolateral prefrontal cortex as "good" or "bad," the orbitofrontal cortex is also in charge of the ability to put aside short-term pleasures for long-term gains (aka higher-order planning), a feeling that "something is wrong here," and the ability to understand what actions are inappropriate.[63] The dorsolateral prefrontal cortex, meanwhile, is responsible for a lack of or reduced impulse control. At the same time, the anterior cingulate cortex—in addition to playing worry-wart, fact-checker, and Monday morning quarterback—is also responsible for tuning into one's own thoughts, whether fully consciously or through meditation.

It is the combined development of these three parts of the frontal lobe—the orbitofrontal cortex, the anterior cingulate cortex, and the dorsolateral prefrontal cortex—that is responsible for the degree to which someone is "mature," as defined by the degree to which they can manifest the same mastery over executive functioning skills as their neurotypical peers. This may explain why we NLDers tend to be noticeably immature with respect to chronological age.

Many experts in the field think that the emotional age of those with NLD is about 75 percent of our chronological age, and my research bears this out. Thus, a 16-year-old would act more like she is 12, and a 20-year-old would have the emotional capabilities of a typical 15-year-old. This is true until the mid- to late 20s, when we start to catch up.

While this may not seem like much of a problem in elementary school (an eight-year-old acting like a six-year-old is not that unusual, and is hard to peg anyway), this age-based discrepancy manifests itself in extremely significant ways. An 18-year-old NLDer who has not yet shown any major teenage rebellion is actually normal. Parents should not think themselves lucky to have "breezed right through" the famous adolescent rebellion, because an 18-year-old with NLD still has the emotional age of about 13.5. So the true "rebellious adolescent" will manifest only when he/she is of college age. Be prepared.

> *My parents had such a hard time with my older siblings during their adolescence, that when I hit 20 and hadn't given them any cause to worry, they thought we all had just sailed right through. Were they surprised to find out that I was just getting started with my so-called teenage rebellion! Looking back, I know I gave them a few rough years there. But everyone goes through the normal stages of development. NLD kids just go through them later.*

Following the same trajectory, we are likely to reach the emotional age of a neurotypical 18-year-old when we are about 24. So this might be the first time we are ready to live away from home in a minimally supervised situation, such as a dorm, with true independent living until the late 20s or even later. This is difficult to hear, both for us and for our parents. And to make it even worse, the world isn't really set up for a 24-year-old to live in a college freshman dorm. Fortunately, as previously discussed, not all executive functioning skills are created equal, and with the right support, we can make significant progress academically once in college. But to prepare for that success, we need to know more about what makes the brain understand different academic functions.

Chapter Eight

NLD and Academics

Why are many NLDers so good at vocabulary, yet bad at reading comprehension? Why might we have poor handwriting? Is it really the case that all NLDers are bad at math? And why does it seem like we can't shut up sometimes? This chapter will cover all of these questions.

Is vocab as easy as A-B-C?

Actually, no. Interpreting speech is hard work. First, you have to have healthy, working ears (which are complex in and of themselves). Then, the sound has to be coded as either familiar enough to pay attention to or not. This process starts in the thalamus and ends in the primary auditory cortex. From there, the sound is coded as either "language" or "not language." If it is language, then it gets sorted out in the language cortex, located in the left hemisphere (about 95% of the time), spread throughout most of the temporal lobe. If it is not language, but instead music, environmental noise, or grunts, groans, screams, or sighs, it goes to a roughly equivalent, though slightly lesser-sized, language cortex in the right hemisphere.

In this sense, the right side is concerned mainly with the "where" of sound, and the left side with the "what" of sound. Since the two hemispheres are connected via the corpus callosum, nowhere stronger than at the temporal lobes, the integration of "what" and "where" is crucial, as it extends not just to identifying sounds, but to a holistic understanding of communication, through linguistic memory, a subset of semantic memory. This semantic memory is concerned with remembering facts and figures, and connects the language cortex with the prefrontal cortex, especially the orbitofrontal cortex, for retrieval. But what, exactly, is going on in the language cortex?

Within the left language cortex, there are a few different important areas. One is Broca's area, named after 19th century French physician Pierre Paul Broca, who treated a patient who could understand both written and oral speech, but could speak only one word ("tan"). When the patient died, the autopsy revealed that he suffered from a lesion in his brain near his left ear. Almost a decade later, German physician Carl Wernicke described a patient with the opposite problem—he could not understand written or oral speech, but he could speak in complete sentences. But because he could not understand what he himself was saying, he often used the wrong words.

Since then, neurologists have determined that Broca's area is not only responsible for language output, but also for grammar and syntax; Wernicke's area, located in the posterior section of the superior-temporal gyrus, is responsible for oral language input as well as converting sounds into words; and a third area, between Wernicke's area and the occipital lode, the angular gyrus, is responsible for written language input. Squished between Wernicke's area and the angular gyrus is the area of the brain responsible for "phonemes" and "graphemes."

These phonemes and graphemes are really the key to understanding dyslexia and dysgraphia.

Decoding dyslexia

Phonemes are individual units of sound. In English, there are 26 letters, but there are about 44 phonemes. For example, the letters "t" and "h" could stand on their own as unique sounds, but "th" could take on either the harder sound of "bath" or the softer sound of "bathe."[64]

There are about three different phonemes per vowel, once dipthongs (sounds formed by combining two vowels into one syllable) are factored in. And in the area between Wernicke's area and the angular gyrus, there are different areas for consonant phonemes and vowel phonemes.

Graphemes are individual units of written language. So it's not just letters that count, but also numbers, punctuation, accents, and other squiggles and lines.

Dyslexia exists when there is a problem converting graphemes to phonemes. Sometimes, the dyslexic student may simply have trouble with word recognition. In this case, the problem is communication between the angular gyrus, which gives letters meaning, and Wernicke's area, which gives words meaning.

Other times, the dyslexic student may see letters backwards or upside down. Here, it's a matter of poor communication between the phoneme area, the angular gyrus, and the visual cortex. It would seem that no matter what, the angular gyrus is at fault. But recent research from MIT (Massachusetts Institute of Technology) shows that the real culprit is a reduction in the arcuate fasciculus, the neural pathway that connects all four major areas in the language cortex (angular gyrus, phoneme area, Wernicke's area, and Broca's area). The looser the connection between Wernicke's area and Broca's area, the study suggests, the smaller the arcuate fasciculus, and the greater the risk of dyslexia.[65]

So, because the arcuate fasciculus connects the functions of reading, writing, grammar, sentence structure, definition, usage, and pronunciation, and commits all of this to semantic memory, the denser these fibers are, the better your general command of vocabulary and language, which may explain why so many NLDers excel in vocabulary.

> I think one of the best days of my life was when I got my highest ever score in Scrabble: 650 points! I just kept hitting it out of the park: BLAZERS with the S making JAMS, GAFFERS with the E intersecting LI, DECENCY making UT into UTE, and perhaps best of all, first INDENTED and then (QI+UN+ID+RE+EN)/QUIRE on top of that down at the bottom left corner. I think when all was said and done, my opponent ended up only with around 270 points, but that was mainly because I got most of the high-scoring letters, and kept on bingo-ing with them.

Reading between the lines

You may wonder why, if you have a good vocabulary, you struggle with reading comprehension.

First, there are the usual problems when reading an assigned book (or any book, for that matter): tiny type and/or vocabulary words that appear rarely, so you are not familiar with them. Assigned reading also trips up everyone at some point, even neurotypicals. Some of the most common difficulties are:

Symbolism: The author may describe the protagonist as waking up on "a gray day." This could mean that it's foggy outside, or it could mean that the author is using the word "gray" to represent old age, weariness, or depression. Granted, one might feel weary or depressed if the weather was bad, but that's not explicit. So how are you supposed to know what the author means? You would have to rely on your understanding of sensory language, as described in Chapter Five.

Flashbacks and "flashforwards": A "jumping timeline" is tough for many NLDers to follow. For example, Chapter One of a novel may be set in the present day; then Chapter Two is set 18 years earlier, when the main characters have not yet met. Then Chapters Three through Five talk about them meeting, then the narrative switches back to the present. This can be very taxing on your dorsolateral prefrontal cortex, where you must put all this information into a cohesive sequence.

> *Sometimes, if I have to read a book that's told in flashback, I actually mark the sections with sticky notes and order them chronologically and then read the book in that order. Otherwise, it makes no sense—I just can't follow it!*

Multiple narrators: Many books, both classic and contemporary, employ parallel narratives and/or narrators, with no one giving "the full story." Each presents his/her own account of what is happening. So while there is some sequencing, this format requires metacognition, all the time.

> *What totally saved me in junior year English is that my older brother told me to read the third section of The Sound and the Fury first, before the rest. Before that, it was just gibberish.*

Cross-referencing and symbolic name dropping: The author makes some passing reference to, for example, the Bible, Shakespeare, Greek mythology, or some other staple of "the classics." If you are not familiar with these references, you would have to stop and look them up. This is a semantic memory issue.

Reevaluation: Your teacher might require you to reexamine the lessons, points, or relevance of what you just read, by asking how a later passage informs what you read in an earlier passage, or vice versa. Having to juggle so much information at once can overload your brain's anterior cingulate cortex. You may ask, "Did I get this right? Did I get any of it right? Can I get anything right?"

So NLDers may struggle with reading comprehension, since it's less about using the language cortex areas, which are assets, and more about using the areas in the prefrontal cortex for executive functioning and social skills simultaneously, which are liabilities.

Reading comprehension tests were the worst. I just can't grasp the main points in any story, but can repeat the details back to you verbatim.

Talking too much

Insofar as the process of deriving meaning from written language relies heavily upon the social understanding and organization areas of the prefrontal cortex, it may help answer one of the most common questions of frustrated parents and teachers: Why don't teens and young adults with NLD *ever* stop arguing? Why do we keep on talking, to the point where the listener sometimes just wants to scream, "I get it. *I get it already!*"

Here's why: if the language cortex areas, temperoparietal junction, and executive functioning brain areas are all working normally, then one could construct a clear, concise, argument. But what exactly prevents you from doing that—from making your point? There are two possible reasons.

One, you could know that there is a point that you are trying to make, but simply can't get the right words out. Specifically, the problem is converting the sequencing of individual letters, phonemes, and words that make up a thought into the sequence of lip movements that represent the thought when spoken. This is indicative of a faulty left pre-motor cortex. Moreover, if instead of trying to convert the thought to a spoken statement, you were to try to convert it to a written one, then this left pre-motor cortex problem would manifest as dysgraphia (described below).[66]

The other possibility is that you are early in the logical sequence of steps that entails making an argument for your (end) point, but your audience has already deduced or inferred what point you are trying to make, and you, being deficient in reading social cues, either haven't noticed this, or cannot understand how the person to whom you are talking has figured out what point is being made if you haven't finished making it yet, and thus you go right on talking, until you are sure that you understand how to arrive at your conclusion, regardless of whether or not your audience is actually still bothering to listen. (See what I mean?) In this case, the part of the brain responsible for this critically important aspect of NLD is the dorsolateral prefrontal cortex.

Speaking, listening, arguing

Speculation though this might be, perhaps the reason many people with NLD have some difficulty speaking extemporaneously is that there might be damage to a connection between the dorsolateral prefrontal cortex, where concepts are formed, and the left pre-motor cortex, which, as previously mentioned, converts the sequence of letters in thought format to spoken-word format or written-word format.

Without having a mastery of this particular aspect of executive functioning, you would lack the internal knowledge to know when, exactly, your point has been made, whereas in the process of making the argument itself, your thinking would be more "strictly logical."

In terms of listening to another person, if your language cortex is working overtime, you might not know when to stop talking. You also might be more likely to nitpick the argument of the person with whom you are conversing because, while you *think* you know what you want to say, you haven't yet gotten your thoughts completely organized. When you listen to someone else, they may be creating a logical, linear argument, proceeding from Point A to Point Z, for example. But if their Point B does not make sense immediately, you may tune out everything else they say and just stick to arguing that one point. You might do this even if, in the process of attempting to refute that point, you don't yet know exactly what you need to say or are going to say. But you have a need to keep talking until your argument makes sense to *you*, which can be really annoying to the other person. Without executive functioning skills, you would sequence your argument aloud until you feel you've made your point sufficiently.

Once the other person grasps that you are not paying attention to anything after their Point B, and they then try to explain that if you would just shut up and listen, you would get it, you might get even more frustrated and angry, even as you wish they would shut up and listen to you. So what started as a conversation and turned into a debate now becomes a fight. (You parents reading this know exactly what I mean!)

Dysgraphia

Dysgraphia, the inability to write coherently, is not actually a complex learning disability. If you have dysgraphia, you may have a hard time writing by hand, with your hand moving too slowly, because the mechanoreceptors in your writing hand and arm aren't working properly. This also may explain why you grip the pencil or pen too tightly. As a result, your handwriting may come out sloppily, slanted, or misspelled. You may have good ideas, and in fact, may be a very good writer indeed, but need extra time to revise what you just wrote in order to get down exactly what you want to say the way you want to say it.

> *When I was in third grade, my teacher told me that my "2s" looked like seagulls flying: that is, they were almost entirely horizontal. In retrospect, I can understand why she said that, but at the time it really hurt my feelings.*

Adding it up: the real deal on math

Ever since Johnson and Mykelbust developed their theory of nonverbal disorders of learning in 1967, there's been an assumption that along with NLD came difficulties with math. The first survey for this book, conducted in 2006, while showing that female NLDers did slightly worse than their male counterparts, disproved that long-held theory that NLDers' math skills will always be below par, and that the discrepancy only widens over time.

Talking about development of "math skills" as though they are homogenous is not useful, since different types of math require very different skills using very different parts of the brain.

Basic arithmetic—the foundation of elementary school math—depends on the intraparietal sulcus and the visual number form area to help determine which of two amounts is larger than the other.[67]

True dyscalculia is the inability to discern which amount is larger than the other. If you have dyscalculia, you may eventually commit to semantic memory the fact that seven minus two equals five, but if you are shown seven objects of equal size and then five of equal size, you couldn't say how many were subtracted. This is solely because you don't have a well-developed intraparietal sulcus.[68]

The order of operations, on the other hand, lies squarely on the shoulders of the dorsolateral prefrontal cortex, since it's just a matter of sequencing. Geometry depends heavily on good visuo-spatial relations skills, found in the back of the parietal lobe near the occipital lobe, while algebraic problems are solved using first the angular gyrus (described earlier) simply to learn how to decipher all those squiggles and lines into a meaningful language of math, as well as the inferior parietal cortex, which is employed in grasping abstract concepts.[69]

Trigonometry and calculus use all of these skills at the same time.

For many NLDers, from elementary school through middle school, math may not be that much of a problem—not until we are presented with abstract problems in algebra. Many of us have found it much easier to take geometry first. Not only does geometry feel more "concrete," but an indirect benefit is that drawing all those shapes and figures may actually help improve dysgraphia.

> I really stunk in math—I got a D in algebra, and was terrified that I would flunk geometry the next semester. It wasn't until my drama teacher took me aside and pointed out that all the Greek plays we were studying actually based their stage design on geometric figures that I began to take an interest. I amazed her, and my math teacher, and even myself, by pulling down a B in geometry!

Other symptoms

Up to this point, we have discussed many of the characteristic traits of NLD, including visuo-spatial problems, the discrepancy between good vocabulary and poor reading comprehension, sensory sensitivity, forgetting to do routine things while needing a routine, missing social cues, hygiene issues, dysgraphia, dyslexia, dyscalculia, panic, and social acceptance, plus multiple aspects of "executive functioning:" impulse control, thinking through how to say something before you say it, scheduling, and "higher-order planning."

This may seem like a comprehensive list, but as the surveys showed, there are other common symptoms of NLD—such as: poor gross motor skills, manifesting as both clumsiness and as an inability to sit without fidgeting; and lack of eye contact—which, whether because they are not "core" symptoms, or they are not absolute, or because there is not enough information available, simply are not discussed here.

Here's what we know for certain about the NLD brain. First, there is a lot more to NLD than a "right hemisphere disorder," because not only does this nomenclature not take into account "executive functioning skills," the roots of which are in various locations throughout the frontal lobe, but it also ignores the fact that everything in the brain is connected. Also, it de-emphasizes the role of the limbic system, not to mention the roles of the various neurotransmitters, a discussion of which is beyond the scope of this book.

Second, it is my belief that there really is no such thing as one "executive functioning disorder" because there are at least seven different facets of "executive functioning," the neurological root of each facet being unique unto itself, even if they all happen to be located in the same general area of the brain (the prefrontal cortex).

But most importantly—parents and teachers, listen up here— *each and every symptom of NLD is neurologically based*, meaning that none of these are made up to frustrate or annoy you. Those of us with NLD are not "lazy," "stupid," "rude," "crazy," "slackers," "spoiled," or "underachievers." We are doing the best we can, given these limitations that we did not choose for ourselves. These real, physical symptoms have a tremendous impact on our mental, emotional, and spiritual health. How do we deal with all this? Read on—you will find out in Chapter Nine.

Part III

What We Want You to Know

Chapter Nine

What We Want Therapists and Guidance Counselors to Know

With all the hard stuff in my life, in the past, I might have cried from everybody dumping on me all the time, now I have become "mature" enough to be really resilient. And yet…sometimes it just gets so damn frustrating, because no one even gives me credit for THAT!

NLD and self-esteem

One of the reasons I wrote this book is that receiving inaccurate information, or sparse information, or no information at all, about NLD can and does affect us negatively. It also affects our families, friends, teachers, and everyone else with whom we come in contact regularly. The extent of the effects can be determined only over time.

Unlike more visible learning disabilities, such as ADHD or Down's Syndrome, NLD is not always immediately apparent, even to a therapist. A stranger may wonder about the slow speech or "immature" social skills. A classmate may wonder about the kid in the next row who is always raising her hand to ask questions or who challenges the teacher on every single point. Well-meaning neighbors may ask the high school student, "So what job are you going to get this summer?" All may not understand that the slow speech, the delayed social skills, the questioning, the inability to work at most jobs available to teens—are not character flaws, they are neurological deficits. Others may think of us as lazy, inept, argumentative, or not trying. All this does is to reinforce how poorly we already may think of ourselves. It underscores how different we are from "normal" neurotypical teens, and makes us feel bad that we can't do what others our age can. In the interviews and surveys, this was heard over and over again:

> *I try really hard. When you have NLD, your brain has to work a lot harder than most people's. I get tired a lot.*

> *You just can't imagine how hard I am working. You think I'm lazy? Try being inside my head for only one day—you'll see how much energy it takes to be me!*

Time after time, encounter after encounter, we are made to feel "less than" by peers, teachers, even family members—for something that is *not* our fault. The longer you and those around you lack clear, accurate information on what NLD is and how to deal with it, the longer the same prejudices and stereotypes will continue. Enough of such encounters, unless counterbalanced by a great number of successes, can easily lead to learned helplessness and even depression.

Is it any surprise, then, that many of us, especially when we are young, have such low self-esteem? From adults, who often don't understand us, we are told we are "troublemakers," "rude" or "stupid" at worst, and "not trying hard enough" or "underachievers" at best. From the adults who do understand, we may hear that our work needs to be edited or supervised, due to our lack of understanding of social norms (such as what is "acceptable" language in an academic paper). It may be well-intentioned help, but it can feel like censorship. From classmates who don't understand NLD, we are called "retards," or "losers," and are viewed as "uncool." Moreover, peers who are mature enough to understand or at least respect our differences are few and far between, and even then, they don't totally "get" us:

> *There was the time in tenth grade when I got a D in sculpture because I just couldn't make anything. And, like, I couldn't form the stuff I was working with at the time into what I wanted...and of course, everybody was like, "You got a D in sculpture?!" 'cause it's an easy class.*

NLD and learned helplessness

> *NLD is SO much more than symptoms. It affects the way we think, it may lead to learned helplessness—which is the psychological term for what*

happens, what you feel when you are perpetually viewed as uncool and so you just stop trying.

In 1967, psychologist Martin Seligman coined the term "learned helplessness," which he describes as "the giving-up reaction, the quitting response that follows from the belief that whatever you do doesn't matter."[70]

In their book *Learned Helplessness*, Christopher Peterson, Steven Maier, and Martin Seligman[71] explain the close parallels between learned helplessness and depression. Of the 19 points used to diagnose depression (combining those of the symptoms, causes, treatments, and prevention), 13 match exactly with the facets of learned helplessness, and an additional five are paraphrased equivalents. This means that there is a 95 percent correlation between the diagnoses of learned helplessness and depression.

> *I feel like I have all these deficits that I am just NOT going to be able to surmount! I feel like everything that I do could easily be interpreted by the world as being less substantive, less creative, less empathic, less intuitive, more pedantic, and more automatonic than the average population. I feel like no matter where I go, I'll never be able to connect with anyone (truly).*

> *To others, I seem "clueless" and "incompetent" (their words, not mine). It's not a treatable condition, and I don't think my life can improve far beyond its current state. I can't expect any support from family members, teachers or peers, who would (and have) immediately dismiss it as a stupid excuse.*

NLD and therapy

> *You might understand the clinical aspects of NLD but you can't possibly know what it's like to live with it.*

Because we have failed so often in the past, we may be very hesitant to seek professional help from a therapist or counselor, even when it might be useful. Sometimes, when you parents don't have answers to these questions or others, you might turn to therapists or to school guidance counselors as a resource, or to seek help for your teen with NLD. We understand that you are trying to be helpful, and we certainly are not saying that all therapy is not useful. However, a lot of us have had less-than-optimal experiences with therapy, and so have very strong negative feelings about it.

Respondents who mentioned being in therapy either disliked or mistrusted (or both) at least one or more past therapists. Looking back, we wish our therapists were more helpful:

> *I couldn't deal with somebody who was bad at being understanding, who was just not a good psychologist...this guy tried to placate kids with teddy bears and shit. But he didn't try to make kids feel at ease...you gotta choose somebody who's going to make an NLD student feel at ease. Because I was emotionally tough, you know—I don't know if emotional sensitivity is part of the NLD, or a difficulty dealing with emotions, not necessarily sensitivity. But whatever, there should be a psychologist that deals with that...*

> *In all the so-called expertise, advancing through their psychology major and degrees, they don't have that much actual experience with either having a learning disability themselves, or living with someone with a learning disability, or even having a large number of LD patients... They really should know that a LOT of the classical training—especially the Piaget— that they teach you in child development is absolutely not useful at all if you have NLD.*

> *[Therapists should] not be so excessively assuming, like, someone assuming "oh, you just had a bad childhood" or that it's some psychological defense mechanism, or anything like that.*

> *Well, I've never been really honest with my specialists. Always like...I am being honest with you [the interviewer], but when I was a kid, it just didn't seem worth the effort to tell these people the real truth.*

The survey asked, "If you could tell therapists, psychologists, doctors and counselors one thing that they should know about NLD, what would that be?" The respondents were not shy about speaking their minds:

NLD is real—you may not be familiar with it, but it is real

> *[NLD] exists, please look for it.*

Please recognize this disorder and provide help to those that need it. If NLD was more widely accepted and well known, my life would be a lot easier.

I'm not sure…that they were looking at my disability from the wrong angle, I guess.

Stop saying we "have ADD," and take the time to learn more about NLD and how it should not be classified as something it is not.

[You] can't change me.

It's not like other more well-known learning disabilities. It is a constant problem in everyday life.

Either NLD is a real diagnosis or it isn't, but you can't have it both ways and just leave me with this scarlet letter that neither of us can fully explain.

Don't be misled by how well we appear to be doing

If everything appears to be all right, that doesn't mean that it is. As a student with NLD, I am very good at hiding how I feel. I don't think that is a choice.

Just because I can do something in the testing room, it does not mean that I can apply that skill in real life.

It's not as concrete as it seems.

Understand that we are very literal learners, and adapt your treatment accordingly

Please speak to me directly and say what you feel.

Create small steps in a learning process and repeat these steps over and over again until the person gets it. Then move on to a following step.

I need more time with you. I need your flexibility. I need you to take the extra steps I cannot see, ask the questions I do not know to ask… I need you to lead.

Please see me as an individual, not just as your patient

Just because we're not developing according to the normal theories of development does not mean that there is anything wrong with us. Also, that before you go labeling, you really have to stop and consider: is there such a thing as a "normal" brain or an "ideal" brain?

Stop theorizing all over me. I am a person, not a case in a textbook. Just because you had another patient some time ago with NLD doesn't make me just like them.

Pay attention to girls before slapping a diagnosis on them. I could have gotten so much more support earlier on.

We are smarter than we seem.

Therapy can be absolute torture for people with NLD if their therapist isn't very well versed in aphasia and other learning disabilities. We are not being non-compliant, we just don't either understand your methods of communication, or are unable to communicate with you.

Finding a therapist who is right for NLDers

Like other kinds of referrals, the most effective way to find a good therapist is to ask other people with NLD who have had a good experience in therapy and who are satisfied with their therapist. If you don't know anyone to ask, you can try getting a referral from your family doctor, if he or she is sufficiently familiar with you and the issues raised by having NLD. For most of us who have health insurance, the choice of therapist will be informed by which therapists are included in the insurance company's network (otherwise, the insurance company will not pay for therapy).

Most insurance companies will provide a list of therapists, sorted by location and specialty. Usually, if you see among the specialties "ADHD," "learning disabilities," or "autism," these therapists may be more likely to have an understanding of NLD. But the best bet is to call and ask. Even then, as you've just read, there are many therapists who just are not effective for us and/or who do not understand NLD at all.

Before you commit to therapy, I highly recommend that you pick up a copy of *Asperger Syndrome and Anxiety* by Dr. Nick Dubin,[72] so you know how to talk about your issues in an effective way. Chapter Seven of his book answers the question at hand, of how to find a therapist that is right for you. But you first should read Chapters Three and Four so you know what kind of therapy may be appropriate. The rest of his book gives good explanations of how various situations may provoke or alleviate anxiety in people with Asperger's, including providing insight into how meltdowns are not entirely bad, but may actually be helpful. Overall, this book is an excellent resource for NLDers struggling with fear and anxiety.

The right therapist at the right time can make a lot of difference for your well-being. If therapy is for you, take time to get a good match. Ultimately, whether you realize that the reasons you originally went into therapy may no longer apply, or you have a breakthrough, or you simply decide that therapy is no longer worth it, understand that you are not alone and that it is not always your fault.

Chapter Ten

What We Want Teachers and School Administrators to Know

It's the beginning of another school year. The back-to-school shopping is done, parents are ready for the hectic schedules, driving children to their various activities, and picking up the pace after a languid summer.

For children, it's just back to homework, back to books, back to teachers' dirty looks. But for nearly one-fifth of the student body, back to school can mean fear, resignation, and dread.

Twenty-two years ago, a naïve but very bright boy started seventh grade. He was ready—sort of—because he'd already seen the year before what middle school could bring. Imagine a 12-year-old kid who's known all of his school life that he's "less than," having been utterly confused by the rules of school beginning back in kindergarten, and who was exiled to the SPED classroom shortly thereafter.

Throughout elementary school, this boy was castigated, thought to be stupid or odd by his peers and teachers, could not write legibly, and had a horrible time reading, and trouble sitting still, all because of his learning disability.

He (and his beleaguered parents) had to sit through countless IEP meetings, where the list of goals read more like a list of New Year's resolutions written by a CEO ("Michael will improve his handwriting 85 percent in four out of five instances"—what?).

Entering middle school meant meeting the SPED kids from all over town, who, though all bullied and teased by the "normal" students, shortly organized themselves into a hierarchy. Recognized learning disabilities (dyslexia and ADHD) were at the top. Autistic and Down's Syndrome kids were off limits because they were defenseless. Everyone else was fair game. That left our hero, as yet undiagnosed, as one of the prime whipping boys.

He knew that, as soon as lunch recess began, he'd be out on the field, being dared by—and usually failing to meet—the challenges of the other kids. It didn't matter what their beef was that day. Watching an NFC game instead of the Patriots? Gut punch. Listening to the wrong kind of music? Bloody nose. Wearing the "wrong" clothes? Body slam. Every single day.

And this was in the days before cyberbullying.

NLD, learned helplessness, and the classroom

Many classroom teachers are inclined to view us as "difficult"—not necessarily troublemakers, but hard to handle. What they may not realize is that we are having a much tougher time than they could ever imagine. For NLDers, the entire school experience can be one of frustration, barriers, and shame.

We may need to do an assignment more slowly, or differently than others. This gets labeled as "uncooperative."

We are likely to get lost in the halls, and are told we are "inattentive."

We speak out of turn, and are scolded for being "disruptive."

We inadvertently may upset the process of the academic system by saying what is on our minds, without editing, or by asking too many questions, and are punished for being "rude," "defiant," or "disrespectful."

We don't mean to be uncooperative, inattentive, disruptive, or rude; we are just trying to make sense of what for us is a difficult and often confusing environment. When we not only don't get the answers we are seeking, but also are put down just for asking the uestions, we feel more and more helpless. Eventually, we stop asking. Add to this how we get socially shunted aside, are teased, and have few opportunities to participate in the school's "normal" social life. No wonder we may feel depressed, sad, and lonely.

I'll never be normal, so why bother.

Please understand how terrible I feel about myself. I have no self-esteem and can't play the sports others can or even write my name or use the scissors correctly.

I'm not being defiant or playing dumb. I am actually struggling here! I may seem articulate but I am very lost in some areas. Stop treating me like this is a behavior problem!

Because NLD is so varied in its symptoms and is so hard to diagnose, other students make fun of us. Sometimes the teasing comes from their own frustration, because they cannot understand how to relate to us when we don't know how to relate to them. Our helplessness is reinforced every day. So we may either retreat into a shell or, conversely, try to get attention by showing off, in order to achieve an identity within our peer group.

Everyone in the Special Ed class in elementary school and middle school was teased on the basis of their being part of the "retard class." I know I was beat up in middle school virtually every single day at recess...not because I was really weak, but because I was kind of acting stupid, so to speak. I mean in terms of not knowing how to be cool.

Talk about lack of impulse control! I was making a total jackass out of myself in high school...[I experienced] this kind of social ostracism. It really didn't manifest fully until high school. I started to become kind of a class clown in middle school, as a result of getting picked on, and I tried to some extent to please the people who were picking on me. But then in high school, I tried to escape that by hanging out with the guys who were two classes ahead of me. It would start out that I would just take certain dares—sometimes to get a dollar or something, and sometimes just for laughs. Usually the bet started out sort of benign, like, do you think you could...?" A typical one might be: "How many packets of McDonald's ketchup do you think you could eat without making yourself sick?" But then, the antics started to turn into things like pulling the fire alarm, playing hooky, and TP-ing [toilet papering] trees. The thing was, I just wanted to be protected from my former bullies, and in the process, try to fit in, someway, somehow. Instead, I earned the most suspensions in the history of the school.

I can honestly say that if there isn't early and accurate identification there really isn't a whole lot that could be said that would be of any true assistance.

It is no wonder that learned helplessness is reinforced once an NLD student is assigned to SPED. Your classmates start teasing you. You may find others in the SPED class who have more recognizable learning disabilities (such as dyslexia or ADD) who tease you too, because even they cannot figure out what your learning disability is.

SPED students are put down by everyone in school. And there is even a hierarchy within SPED classes, wherein the NLD student is at the bottom. Because even if someone has Down's Syndrome or other form of retardation, the others in SPED know what that is and how to deal with it.

There really seems to be a pecking order in school. In the early grades, everyone else puts down the SPED students. They call us "the kids on the short bus." The "in group" of diagnosable LD students might very well put down the un-diagnosable or just plain "weird" children.

…not only do we end up getting ostracized among our "normal" peers, but there is so much emphasis these days on other, trendier learning disabilities that you could have. I know that these days, ADD is so cool, now autism is up-and-coming and it's very chic to have it, but there doesn't seem to be any real help…if you have NLD.

Nevertheless, by middle school, learning disability students often put aside our own differences and band together in sympathy. We may become our own social clique, which in turn can make it difficult to interact with any other group.

Social interaction in school

Not understanding the rules of social interaction in school is a serious detriment to those of us with NLD. When we were younger, our parents, siblings, and teachers probably watched out for us, and prevented us from making total fools of ourselves. Now that we are older, we have to learn to do this for ourselves. It really can be difficult when we don't "get" the unwritten rules our peers somehow seem to intuit. In school or in social interactions, we may speak out of turn, ask questions that others consider inappropriate, and generally disrupt the learning process, even though we do not intend to be rude or disobedient.

> *In fourth grade, our class took a field trip to Orchard House in Concord—the home of the Alcotts and the place where Louisa May wrote Little Women. We were greeted at the door by a gentle older woman in 19th-century dress, who welcomed us by saying, "Hello children. I am Marmee, Louisa May's mother. I am so glad you could visit our home." I knew she wasn't telling the truth. Marmee lived in the 1800s and this was 1990. As she spoke, I grew more and more uncomfortable and confused. I knew that lying is wrong. And she was definitely not telling the truth. I was angry, I didn't know why someone was lying to me, not just about her name, but also about the fact that she could pretend to be something she wasn't. Finally, I couldn't take it anymore, and much to the chagrin of my class and teacher, I decided it was time to reveal the truth. "You're not the real Marmee!" I shouted, and my teacher led me out of the room. I was so angry that I was being censured for telling the truth. Truth is very important to me. I felt betrayed.*

What could the teacher have done ahead of time to prevent this situation? She could have said, "When we go on the field trip tomorrow, there will be an actress who will be playing the part of Marmee. As part of her acting role, she may even say she is Marmee, so don't let it throw you, she isn't lying, she is acting, and that is OK." The problem is, though, that unless we were in a very small class, and the teacher knew us very well, she probably couldn't have anticipated this in advance.

We know you may be frustrated teaching us. But please don't ever resort to physical tactics, or to shunting us off to guidance counselors because you don't know what else to do. There usually is another way.

> *I started to zone out, especially during math and physics classes, and the teacher took me by the head and asked me to pay attention. (Gestures the teacher shaking him.) Well, not like shook me or anything, just held me by the head (laughs). Ya' know, I felt like it was a loss of control, and I sort of liked that teacher, except for when he was a jerk...*

Hello! (to teacher) It's YOU who needs to be guidance counseled, not me. Just because YOU don't get how I learn, doesn't mean there is anything wrong with me.

So how *can* teachers help the student with NLD? The survey asked, "If you could tell your grade school (K-12) teachers one thing they should know about NLD, what would that be?" The respondents had plenty to say.

What we want our teachers to know

[Teachers] should not assume that we're deliberately being stubborn or socially clumsy, or any way someone could negatively perceive us...when somebody has these kinds of issues, it's not something deliberate...teachers should not whip through explanations of topics too fast. And often, students with learning disabilities take a longer time to really absorb the information, and if she just whips through it, the student may not pick up on something highly crucial.

I have never really had any teachers who I got very close to.

We *are* working hard!

Do not tell me, "You need to try harder."

Show compassion.

This really is my best work. I'm not being lazy when I turn in a paper three pages shorter than assigned.

You have no idea how hard my brain was working. You kept telling me I wasn't trying but I was, I really was!

I'm not lazy, this is just who I am. I need all the help I can get.

NLD people work really, really hard, even if you can't see it!!!

Be patient. Please, for the love of God, be patient with me. Also, never ever give me another journal assignment again. Those are torture.

Forget all your theories—please teach us using methods that will help us learn

Teach me verbally!

Create ways to talk about the information being presented. In math classes, have the students talk out the reasons for completing each step.

Be very straightforward with all that you tell and ask students with NLD.

[Recognize] that I need things said verbally. If things aren't said verbally, I will not understand.

If a child is rude, they do not mean to be. Please do not punish them. Also, please teach kids with NLD that it is OK to tattle. I'm 23, and I still have nightmares about middle and high school because I thought it was wrong to rat on the bullies.

Please make time to learn more about NLD

You really "can" get As in advanced reading and Cs in slow math, and it's not because of laziness.

I don't care how smart you think I am. I am doing the best I can.

Get training and be honest with parents about the fact that you are not medical professionals, your goal is to educate, not treat, these conditions.

Don't jump to conclusions about students and their abilities, and for God's sake, get over yourselves.

You don't get us, so stop pretending you know all about NLD.

It is real.

Educate people as best you can about it, that not everybody that has an NLD is the same. When I was in school there was an "understanding disabilities" class and never once was anything like Asperger's or NLD mentioned.

Think outside the box.

In grades K–6 watch [for the signs of NLD]: [poor] handwriting, reading beyond grade level. In grades 7–12, [watch for] learning style.

[In terms of] test taking, present tests that are similar to the homework so we know what to expect.

Give me less work.

Don't give up. Take your time. Don't judge.

Read Michael Brian Murphy's book!

We SPED kids are not nutcases, or even, the vast majority of the time, retarded, just INCONVENIENT for you to deal with.

If I show you that I can do one math problem, I don't need to do 100 a night. Five maybe, but not 100. You can't imagine how long this takes me.

Just because I am not taking notes does not mean I don't hear what you are saying.

We need and deserve your respect

We may feel that we don't want to even bother trying in classrooms with teachers who don't understand us and who see us as incompetent.

The teachers that were unprepared to be teachers, the ones that are in public schools now, should know that if they weren't prepared for an NLD student, they shouldn't even try, because they're just not going to do a good job. And with teachers who actually care, and who actually have looked into what an NLD student needs, they should know that—usually I have wanted to make an effort, though it might not seem like it. When a teacher studies what NLD is, that's different from actually encountering a student or a person with NLD.

Our frustration may be aimed not at the teachers, but more at the administration

I'm not going to need sculpture in my life. I would like it in my life, but if it's not there, then that's fine. I don't need to have this…art in my diploma. It's not something that is necessary for people coming from your school to have. It's not something anybody's going to look for…up there, like, really going over my education with a fine tooth comb, they're not gonna look and say, "Oh, no! This school doesn't have any kind of art requirements. We don't know if there's any kind of art in his history. We can't hire him. It's just, it's just pointless.

We don't just have a learning disability—we are individuals too!

[We] can do anything normal kids can do, even if it takes longer, and [you need] to recognize the different learning style. Allow us to take classes that we are motivated to take, like taking a foreign language.

Not everybody learns the same way. Don't treat any students as if they are stupid when they don't respond to "hidden curriculum" subject areas. They and YOU might not know they have a learning disability.

[Answering] this one is very emotional for me because I rarely understood verbal instructions presented quickly to the class. I always needed examples which were presented when I made my way to the teacher's desk after everyone else started the assignment or test. For years, you ask yourself why it is you simply cannot understand so easily like everyone else. I wish the teachers could have understood that "I learned differently."

Give us more options to learn and don't force us to be "normal."

Don't treat it like a sentence, it's just a learning difference.

Teachers and administrators: don't assume that we are all bad in math, or good in English, just because that's what you've read in the NLD literature. We are as varied as any other students in the classes we like and dislike, and in which we do well or poorly. The survey asked, "Was there a class in grade school that was a total waste of time?" We said:

Religion.

Math (I didn't get it), arts and PE (I couldn't do it.)

Gym class.

Algebra. Latin.

Chorus. I don't think I can despise chorus enough.

Gym, social studies, language.

Maybe "family life" class in middle school. (A lot of people without disabilities would probably agree with me, though ;-)).

Any class that didn't verbalize the curriculum.

Gym. I hated it and it hated me right back. It was pure torture. Also, I couldn't learn languages, so I don't know why my parents had me switch them—I flunked Spanish as badly as I flunked Latin.

Nothing was a waste of time, difficulty in gym class and art class.

Algebra and Latin.

And, on a more positive note:

> *Not really. I was interested in learning, even when I wasn't too good at it.*

> *When teachers do take the time to learn about NLD, they can and do make a difference in our lives.*

Teachers: you absolutely have the ability to change our lives for the better!

In an ideal world—where funding for education is limitless and all teachers are enlightened enough to embrace the concept of many kinds of learners with many kinds of learning styles, and where every single public school student actually has an IEP (the most democratic approach to school), there would be no learning disabilities, only, perhaps, teaching disabilities. But in our less-than-perfect system of public education, what can one teacher do?

> *The things we struggle with are real, and our struggles are often unnoticed. Look for the signs, because the entire direction of a child's life can be changed if the appropriate interventions are made.*

A teacher who takes the time to notice, who makes the time to help, can have long-lasting, life-changing effects. The survey asked, "Have you had any teachers who changed your life for the better? If so, please tell us about one." The respondents were enthusiastic about the good, caring teachers they had:

> *Yes, despite not knowing about my NLD, I had teachers who saw my potential and spent extra time helping me grow as a student and person. I appreciate that.*

> *My Dutch [language] teacher in high school had personal conversations with me and kept on telling me that I meant something. He also helped me with small tasks, not doing them for me, but giving me tools to accomplish them myself.*

> *The teacher I had for the last half of first grade accepted me and made me feel pride in myself for the first time and I think about that a lot.*

An English professor in college actually critiqued my writing and taught me a lot about the craft. Most of my teachers before then just figured I was a good writer who they didn't have to teach at all.

One teacher who stands out is Mr. K., my sixth grade English teacher. He is the first one who taught us how to actually write. Whatever you do, you have to make sure you know your topic, voice, and audience. Everything else is just busy work.

Yes, I have had several wonderful teachers. The commonality is that they care—they care about their work, they care about teaching, they care about you learning, and they care about you succeeding no matter how much effort it takes on their part.

Ms. P., my drama teacher in college, and Ms. E., my voice teacher in college. Ms. E. helped me become more self-aware and both of them did not mind that I am quirky.

[My] second grade Special Ed teacher Miss B. She tried the hardest and gave me hope.

Yes, I had a math teacher who took the time to learn with me. We had no idea about the NLD at this point, but she took the time to make sure I understood everything.

My ninth grade history teacher was just out of college and I felt that I had a connection to her. She was a mentor all throughout my high school years and helped me with everything.

Yes, the teachers who changed my life were the ones who "got" me when no one else did.

One math teacher knew I just couldn't do math and he let me pass if I wrote him a poem about math instead of doing the problems. It probably wasn't ethical but I was a good student otherwise and he knew that failing me would ruin my chances for college.

Mrs. Rose, my eighth grade music teacher, saw my creative side and encouraged me to continue playing the piano, even though I flunked band (trying to play the tuba). Now, how many people do you know who actually flunked band? It is due to her that I am still a musician today. Otherwise, I would have been too discouraged to continue.

Yes. Teachers who genuinely cared and showed that they did. Teachers who hugged me during a meltdown. Teachers who praised me—I lived for praise. Teachers who let me use their room to eat lunch in or cool down when I needed a break.

Teachers who care about us, who see us as individuals, not just as "problem children," who are willing to take the time to help us learn, and who are willing to work together with our parents, can make or break our entire school experience. Parents who understand us and are willing to work cooperatively with teachers and school administrators make up the other half of our academic support team. Parents, how can you be effective?

Chapter Eleven

Talking to Parents about NLD

It is crucial for parents and teachers to know exactly what is wrong, and more often, what is right, with their child or student. It is even more crucial for the NLD student to know exactly what is "wrong" and "right" with him or herself.

Having NLD affects not only the individual, but the whole family as well. A teen with NLD who is angry or confused can upset the whole family dynamic, whereas one who is calm and happy can affect the family for the better.

One way to keep the peace is to make sure that the household runs smoothly, in an orderly fashion, and with as little disruption as possible. Some of the ways we have found that work well follow.

Tell your teen exactly what his or her household responsibilities and chores are, when he or she needs to do them, and critically important—what constitutes a good job!

I'm very literal, and logical... I need a lot of things explained to me very, very, very explicitly... I think that kind of annoys some of the people I live with... There have been many times while I was growing up, if my mom said to me "do the dishes," I do just that: I empty the dishwasher, load it again, and leave. And she might get upset with me, because it was "ever-so-obvious" that I had to not only empty and load it, but also clean out the sink and clean up the counters, and then rinse out the sponge. As if that were somehow implied.

We find it really, really helps to have a printed list posted somewhere where your teen can see it.

If it's not written down, it's not gonna happen!

Post a written meal plan for the week on the refrigerator. This helps in two ways: one, if your teen knows what is planned for dinner, he or she is less likely to snack on one of the main dinner ingredients. And two, if your teen is responsible for doing some of the meal preparation and cooking for the family, he or she then knows exactly what's for dinner, without having to plan it.

Cooking is easy and fun—but deciding what to make for dinner is just about impossible!

Household rules concerning things like homework time and bedtime, limits on TV, radio, video games, internet, and cell phone use, etc. should be discussed, explained logically, and probably written down somewhere.

Teens should be included in family discussions, and where appropriate, their opinions should be taken into consideration in major family decisions.

By the time we are in high school, we should get to help decide where we go on our summer vacation. I am so tired of my parents treating me like a baby and saying, "We're going to the beach again," when my best friend's family lives in our old hometown and I really would much rather spend some time with him.

It was really horrible when my collie Sheila broke her leg. My parents wanted to take her to the vet to put her down, but I wanted the vet to try to do surgery first. I mean, we got her when I was in kindergarten and she was pretty much my best friend. Then I found out it was going to cost more than $3,000 to do the surgery, and it might not even work that well. My parents didn't want to pay that much money for an old dog. I said I would use my college fund and they finally said I could. But the vet told me that Sheila really wouldn't ever recover, and that it was better for her not to have to suffer. But after a couple of days of watching Sheila limp around all groggy from painkillers, I finally had to agree that she should be put to sleep.

I can understand that my parents sometimes have to make major decisions for the family. When it was time to paint the house, I helped choose the colors for the family room and kitchen, and I had complete control over the colors for my new room.

Remember that we don't like change. Because most NLDers do not adapt easily or happily to change, one of the most helpful things parents can do to make family life easier is to explain clearly in advance, whenever possible, any changes in routine or family life that may be imminent.

For example, remember the story about the teen who was so upset when his parents replaced the track lighting in the living room that he actually broke down and cried? What could his parents have done to help avoid that? The conversation could go something like this:

> Son, we are going to make some changes in our living room next week, and we want to tell you why. Just like clothes go in and out of fashion, so do lighting fixtures. When we installed it, the track lighting that we now have was very stylish. But now, years later, it looks dated and we want to replace it with more modern recessed lighting. Plus, the track lights make the room very hot in the summer, as you know.

> So we have picked out some new fixtures. Here's a brochure that shows what they will look like. Mr. Johnson, the electrician, will be coming over when you get home from school next Tuesday. He will take out the old lights and install the new ones for us.

> We know that these lights have been here ever since you can remember, and that this change will be upsetting for you. But these are our reasons and we hope that soon, you will enjoy our attractive new lights too.

What are the important elements of this little speech?

- Inform your teen ahead of time so he or she can prepare intellectually for the change.

- Explain the need for the change logically (in this case, there are two reasons).

- Inform him/her either that you already have made a final decision (as in this case) or that his/her input will be welcomed, if appropriate.

- Acknowledge that he/she feels upset about the change.

- Reassure him/her that he/she probably will be happy with the new results in a short time.

My parents taught me that in our house we follow the Golden Rule: "The one who has the gold makes the rules!" I didn't understand this when I was younger, until they explained that "gold" meant "money" and that the one who is putting up the money for something gets to decide what to buy.

"Because I said so"—NOT!

The worst thing parents can tell a NLD teen is: "because I said so." That just drives us crazy with frustration. We are not being defiant. We really need a logical reason for what you are asking us to do. Honestly.

Parents, should you ever think of using the line "because I said so" with your NLD teen, *don't*. Maybe you read a child development book written for "normal" neurotypical children, which says that children will grasp the idea that parents have a right to say "because I said so" by virtue of their position of authority and responsibility in the family. The child or teen, being a child and not an adult, needs to learn that when a parent speaks, he or she must obey.

And maybe that is true for a neurotypical child or teen. But because of the way our brains are wired, we will not respect you based solely on your authority, at least not until we reach our mid-twenties to early thirties, and by then we will no longer need your daily guidance.

NLDers either have no idea what the "because I said so" line means, or we think we know exactly what it means ("you feel the need to use your authority to coerce us into doing what you want"). In either case, we can't conceive of why doing something "because you said so" is in any way important or significant *to us*. Instead, we will look at you, mystified, wondering why you would say something so irrational, and also wonder why you are wasting your time or ours.

Here is a helpful hint. If it is absolutely necessary that you must use the "because I said so" line on your NLD teen, it would be a good idea first to explain what "because I said so" actually means. Better yet, to save you both the time and energy, before you tell us to do the chore or task in question, tell us first that there will be a break in the ordinary, daily schedule that necessitates doing that particular chore or task.

An example might be: "I get really upset and frankly, kind of nauseated, when I look at your messy room. I know you don't want me to go in there and barf on your books and CDs—so go clean it up!"

Or another: "Grandma and Grandpa are coming over, and I want your room to look clean to please them. Because they are my parents, it makes me feel bad when they think I'm not an effective parent to you." Contrast these two reasons with: "Clean your room because I said so."

Another example is: "It's going to rain tonight, so you need to mow the lawn today instead of tomorrow, when the grass will be too wet to cut," as opposed to just, "Mow the lawn now (because I said so)."

Here are some other typical parental remarks to avoid, as they are futile and will be lost on your NLDer:

- "I'm only doing this for your own good."

- "I said NOW!"

- "If everyone jumped off a bridge, would you do it too?"

- "Go to your room."

- "I don't care what Cindy's mother lets her do."

- "Act your age."

- "Grow up."

- "You'll thank me later for this."

- "This hurts me more than it hurts you."

- And many others.

Yes, we know it takes more of your time to explain things, but think of all the time you'll save by not having to engage in incessant arguing!

So what can you do to maintain order in your household? How can you effectively guide, instruct, or—when necessary—discipline your child or teen with NLD?

The survey asked, "What suggestions would you give to parents of young NLDers in terms of effective discipline? What rewards and punishments have been effective for you? What hasn't been effective?"

Here is our best advice:

Explain why you're doing what you're doing. Ask your kid why they did what they did, but ask in a non-accusatory way.

Consult a highly qualified therapist. Don't punish anyone for not understanding your indirect instruction. A close relationship with your children is the most effective form of discipline.

Screaming at us, berating us, and humiliating us don't work and are only counterproductive. We get enough of that crap at school. I would suggest a carrot-only approach, but when you do punish us, ALWAYS make sure we understand that you are being clear, just, and logical.

Use ABA [Applied Behavior Analysis].

I was diagnosed late and so was unable to go through this. But I am inclined to believe positive reinforcement is key.

Be very clear about what you expect of them and why you expect these things. Repeat your expectations after infractions to make sure they are aware of what exactly they did wrong. My NLD was treated as a behavior issue as a child—when I didn't notice a mess somewhere I was "being defiant" by not cleaning up after myself, when I forgot things or didn't understand something I was treated like I was lying and playing dumb. Nothing really worked.

Don't hit if possible because it can send the wrong message that it is OK to hit other kids. Talking helps me a lot to calm down. Also, explain to the person why they are in trouble for doing such and such.

Punishments usually don't work, unless they are very, very logical, and tied to the infraction (e.g. "If you don't clean up your room, you won't get that new poster for your room," not "If you don't clean your room, you won't get to go to your friend's birthday party"). Rewards are more effective.

Positive is better, but they figured it out. [What is not effective is] when they lose patience with me.

Don't try to punish someone by controlling an intense interest.

Punishment-wise, I am not sure. I had such a guilty conscience about everything as a kid. I tortured myself about it. No punishment was usually necessary.

Try to maintain the same tone when disciplining as you would when asking, "How was your day?" We go into a vacuum when something gets even more confusing than it already is on a daily basis.

One respondent sums up this topic nicely:

No real advice here, nothing beyond "be understanding and loving."

Most parents try to be helpful if they can, but wind up just as frustrated or confused as we are, until they learn more about NLD.

Well, sometimes my father is a little surprised at…some of the things I can't do, but it's nothing major. There's not been anything dramatic like that.

I also wish my parents had known about my NLD when I was younger. Since learning about the diagnosis they have been my biggest advocates, but when I was younger they attributed NLD-related issues to lack of effort.

Probably the single most important thing parents can do is *to learn more about NLD* (so thanks for reading this book).

Help, don't hurt

If you—or a family member—don't really understand NLD, the message you (or they) give your NLD teen may not be benign or supportive. One recurrent theme in a family in which one child has some kind of "problem" (certainly not exclusive to families with an NLDer) is that one parent may be (mostly) supportive and understanding, while the other parent is in complete denial that there is even a problem.

Well, my mom is supportive, but she wants me to continue to take—I'm pretty sure it was [name of medication]—but I'm pretty sure it has barely any effect, I mean, I burn too much. So I don't want to take it anymore. So that's the only thing we disagree on. The strange thing is, it's also an anti-depressant, but &#$% that. My dad, on the other hand, doesn't really want me to…never wanted to accept that I had NLD. My dad is *willing to help me any way he can, but if anything new—any new kind of disability crops up, he doesn't want to accept it. Like, I could have Asperger's Syndrome, but he's decided that's an umbrella term that doesn't mean anything, and so I don't have it. So that's my dad's reaction: to be supportive, but wanting to deny, you know.*

To their teen, parents often either respond with, "We're getting you help, getting you into special education classes," or "We're getting you a therapist," or sometimes, even worse, "What's *wrong* with you? Why can't you just behave yourself?"

It's really hard sometimes, when you have NLD and even your own family doesn't get it. My father for example, yells at me all the time to try harder. Once he sent an email which said, "My goal is to have [you] free of the need for LD status…the time is good for [you] to move to be fully normalized (sic)." As if!

Siblings and family members

When it comes to siblings and extended family members, they also may not understand much about NLD.

I have a half-sister who is much older than I am, and I don't think she knows. Beyond my parents, nobody really knows because it was never really important until last year when I actually had a name for something.

My brother really doesn't get it. He just gets embarrassed when I do socially awkward things at school. But, you know, he will still stick up for me if the other kids tease me. It really helps to know he loves me, even if he doesn't always understand that I can't help it.

Some siblings know a little about NLD, but may "wish it away:"

Well, I mean, I really don't want to talk about it…but the immediate family member who upsets me the most though is my sister, who is not in denial that I have a problem, but she doesn't want me to confront my father about the fact that there is something wrong with me that cannot be fixed. She doesn't want me to confront him because she doesn't want to cause trouble. And because she's my sister, that really troubles me. I mean I wouldn't just go out and tell her, "There's only one way that this can be resolved, and that's for me to tell him either to accept me or go take a hike."

But I really just don't like the fact that usually she takes no side at all, and if she takes a side, it's always his.

But siblings also can be our best friends and champions:

My brother is two years older than me, and he actually punched a kid who was teasing me in the cafeteria. I was sad 'cause he got in trouble with the principal, but you know—they stopped teasing me!'

My sister is really the one person I can always count on to help and to listen.

What we want our parents to know

Parents, whether or not you understood the information in Chapters Four through Eight about neural connections and language is not as important as *understanding that we do not argue with you merely to drive you crazy*. Rather, it is because we are really confused by the myriad of what are to us illogical rules and inconsistencies and to which we are expected to conform.

[I wish my parents had known] that I wasn't being difficult on purpose.

I do believe it might have been helpful for my parents to have kept more of an open dialogue about my NLD than they had.

[I wish my parents had known] that I was not a lazy ass.

Please be more patient with me, it takes me longer to learn social skills.

You say that everything I do in life is a decision, but I did not decide to be born, much less be born with disabilities. Nor for that matter, did I decide where to live, what school system to go to, nor what the greater arc of my life was going to look like.

[NLD] is a real thing that is causing significant difficulties!

Don't decide my future for me.

You may not understand it completely (or at all) but that doesn't mean it isn't real.

I'm trying. Really.

Be more mindful of the fact that physical symptoms come along with the stress of having an NLD, which is why things that appear common sense can sometimes be avoided.

Just because I don't seem to understand or identify what is being said does not mean I am not listening. Possibly cogitating.

It did not matter how many times you tried to teach or explain to me something by presenting it slowly or differently, if it was not in the context or in an order my brain was able to process it, it was not going to register. I was not being defiant, but rather overly frustrated and anxious because I was most often not in my comfort zone.

The challenges that I face as a result.

That I work as hard as I can even if I fail.

Our NLD is real and it is not going away. Having NLD is not something we can change about ourselves, though we can make accommodations and compensations for it. In other words, if there is some aspect of NLD in which we improve over time, then great. Otherwise, we hope you can learn to live with it. We certainly have to.

One thing I wish my father knew is that this is me, and you can't just wish it away. The thing I wish my mother had known is that I had NLD, and that means I would be living at home a lot longer than she'd planned for when she had me.

I don't think my parents knew anything about learning disabilities. I think schools and teachers need to undergo more training in LD so they are better able to identify problems in students and to refer their families to appropriate professionals.

I wish my father would understand that I am not making this up. My mother is pretty good about getting it, and helps me any way she can.

That I had it, and home and school would have not been so frustrating. If my parents knew I had a different learning style, they could have taught me things in a different way, so it wouldn't have been so frustrating for everyone.

Because our NLD is here to stay, it is imperative that you, the parent, do your best to understand us and NLD. But for heaven's sake, *don't baby us.*

> *When I first got to high school and we had just found out I had NLD, my mom wanted to hand out these little pamphlets she had printed up to all my teachers, explaining NLD and how they could help me. This was SO incredibly embarrassing. I didn't want to hurt her feelings, so I just chucked them all in the wastebasket the minute I got to school.*

Instead, help us *build on our strengths*:

> *I wish they had pushed me to get involved in the community more.*

> *[I wish my parents had known] how smart I was.*

> *[I wish my parents had known] that maybe we could've found a different way to do my physical therapy, because touching my left leg felt really uncomfortable when I was younger, and I would laugh (it was like tickling, but not quite), and my mom would laugh.*

> *[I wish my parents had known] that I just can't do everything everyone else can.*

And please help us to understand the nuances of things that may seem obvious to others our age. In addition to not understanding the rules of social interaction, unlike most kids, teens with NLD often do not absorb the norms of our culture except through direct experience. This is why we often need a parent or other adult to "interpret" the rules for us.

> *One day when I was 15 and had just come home from school, the little boy next door rang the bell. He and his friend wanted to come in and play with our cat, as he and his little sister often did. "Sure," I told him, and let them in and went back downstairs where I was doing my homework. I forgot all about them, until about an hour later when the doorbell rang. It was the police. Apparently, he didn't tell his mom that they were going to our house. When the friend's mother came to pick up her son, and the boys couldn't be found, she got hysterical. They called the police. Even though our neighbor told her I was a nice guy, when the lady saw that her five-year-old son had been in the house with a teenager, she went ballistic, and wanted to have me arrested. The police asked me a*

lot of questions, and then called my mother home from work. My mother had to explain to me that there were bad guys who sometimes hurt little boys. That never would have crossed my mind when I was 15. I was so shocked and sad. I would never hurt anyone.

And before you criticize us, *take a look in the mirror*. The survey asked, "Do you think one or both of your (biological) parents may have NLD? Why or why not?"

I think my dad has some NLD tendencies because he lacks some social skills. My mom—I don't think she had NLD nor anything like it.

Yes. My dad is oblivious to the nonverbal communication of others so often.

My mother certainly seems to have some "word nerd" qualities, as well as being anxious and sensory-sensitive to smells, tastes, and is often bothered by labels. My father is somewhat of a narcissist, and quite often is insensitive to other people's feelings, and sometimes doesn't pick up on social cues. But I wouldn't consider either of them full-blown NLDers.

No, not really.

When my parents first found out that there was a vague diagnosis and I sort of explained to them what it was, they—I can remember this so clearly—we were in the car, and I don't remember where we were going, but the two of them were fighting: "It's my fault!" "It's my fault!" kind of thing. It's really kind of funny. And my dad was particularly hard on himself, so I gave him an example of something that someone with NLD might do that definitely would not have come from him…

Both my parents seem a little bit Aspie sometimes.

Not my parents, but I think my uncle might. He is a bit socially inept [I can tell] by some of the questions he will ask me sometimes.

Yes, my dad is weird like me.

No. Although both show some NLD symptoms neither share enough to make that argument.

Interestingly, my dad, who was a college professor, has presented from time to time with NLD-type traits, e.g. "deer in the headlight" look when

I present what I consider simple step-by-step instructions to fix something on the computer.

One parent is slow to process nonverbal things; the other has pretty bad visual and spatial issues.

Yes, my mother is a lot like me but doesn't see it.

Please, when we are too young to stand up for ourselves, help us by *being a buffer* when other family members don't understand. In response to the question, "What would you say to parents or other relatives who believe that NLD isn't real and/or that you're making it up?" we said:

You can believe what you believe, but it's real and makes life very difficult.

F&↗^k you.

NLD may or may not be a real or valid diagnosis, but all of the symptoms are real and not going away.

I probably wouldn't say anything because it seems like no one believes me.

Watch videos on the subject and get informed.

You are wrong. I might say it more rudely though. :)

My parents know it is real and they make sure people know I'm not making it up.

You try having it.

Oh well…

Not nice things. Possibly educational things, but still not said nicely.

I would ask them to close their eyes and imagine being placed on a packed sidewalk, in the middle of Times Square, during Friday rush hour, seeing chaos everywhere, and having absolutely no clue how or what to do and where to go next. It is the practiced NLDer who is able to "center," separate, and go through their own developed processes to navigate them to a safe place. It takes years of practice and discipline, yet know it is their own coping strategies that make it bearable. It will never go away, but rather [be] a bit more tolerable through repetition.

Walk a mile in my shoes. See what I see, hear what I hear, feel what I feel. Then maybe you'll understand how hard it is.

Denial doesn't make the condition go away.

And in answer to the question, "What would you say to a parent of an NLDer who believes that their child 'got the NLD' from the other parent?" we said:

It's not helpful to blame anybody. There's no scientific evidence that NLD is hereditary genetic and not de novo genetic.

F*^k you also. WHO CARES where it came from???

They're your genes, too, you idiot!

That's a tough one.

I would ask them if pointing fingers was helping the child. The child has it and you can't undo that by being a jerk to their other parent. Be a grown up...

Stop blaming. No one knows if it's genetic or not.

Maybe they did, maybe they didn't. What difference does it make?

I can't say anything...unless I know the parents and can make a sound judgment.

HAH HAAAAHAHA Was there only one parent who helped produce that baby?

I would ask: Does it matter? It is really important? How would that change anything?

It's not their fault.

This poignant reply sums it up really well:

It doesn't matter where it came from. It's your child. Love them.

Fortunately, some of our parents actually get it and understand how to help:

I think they did know [what to do to help] and now that I'm older, it is out of their hands completely.

The benefit of being the child of a special education director is that you're immediately subjected to a battery of tests at the first sign of a learning disability. I think they knew everything they needed to know about [having NLD].

And when we are older, please *be aware of bullying.*

If you are the parent of the bullied, the bullies, and those who just stand by, what can you do? Even if you're sure they already know, talk with your children about treating others with respect, especially those who are "different," about what it means to have compassion, and about the fact that bullies are often the kids you'd least expect (most often those who themselves feel marginalized or "less than" in some way).

And if your kid is the one being bullied? Well, chances are good you won't know it—at least not directly. Watch for the signs (bruises, torn clothing, missing lunch money). Ask your child— hypothetically, because for many young teens that's the only way in—"What would you do if you were being bullied?"

Then you have some choices to make. Are you going to insist that your child tells you everything, being oblivious to the fact that when he or she squeals and you tell the school administration, the bullying will double? Good luck with that.

Are you going to support a "zero tolerance" policy that criminalizes good-natured teasing and ribbing, rubber-band shooting, and "yo mama" jokes, and that in one community has led to an arrest for biting a Pop-Tart into the shape of a gun? Are you going to turn a blind eye, saying "boys will be boys," or "the girls will work it all out"? Or chalk it up to "character building"? Are you going to teach your child to walk away and try to ignore it?

Or are you going to show your child how to take a moral stand, defending not just himself or herself but also others who are younger, weaker, or viewed as "less than," and raise your child to fight back by fighting injustice? It's your call. How you are preparing your child to deal with the outside world has a huge impact on his or her social and emotional development.

Social and emotional development

As was already discussed, perhaps the one most critically important fact for parents to keep in mind is the finding that both the social skills and executive functioning skills of a person with NLD typically make us act and react as a neurotypical person about 75 percent of their chronological age would. That is, an 18-year-old with NLD may not be ready to leave home to go to college, but may be just about ready for summer camp.

> *I failed royally at the first college I went to, so the next term, my folks sent me to a college specifically for kids with learning disabilities. Despite the fact that I still failed virtually every class I took, at least I was having a really good time. I was having fun wasting my life away, downloading and playing NES, SNES, and Genesis ROMs on my computer, and subsequently having seizures from playing them nonstop, even though I have photo-sensitive epilepsy, and knew I wasn't supposed to be gaming. Because there were no restrictions on what you could eat or drink, every day, I always got bacon and eggs for breakfast; every night when I went down to the game room, I always ordered buffalo wings and either jalapeño poppers or mozzarella sticks; and I averaged about 5–6 16 oz. glasses of Coke a day. When I first showed up there in the summer of 2000, I weighed 190 lb., but when I was asked to leave in May 2002, I weighed 285 lb. But I was having fun, wasn't I? Every week or so, there was a van to take us to the local cinema, and once a semester, there was some kind of field trip (the best was to the local Six Flags). But despite all of this, I hated my life. I was a fat tub of lard; I had no chance in hell of getting a girlfriend, I was failing most of my classes, I missed my family, and anything resembling the religious services I used to attend at home was completely inaccessible to me. But, at least having to survive some of my roommates helped me improve my social skills!*

NLD and learned helplessness at home

After a lifetime of missing social cues, messing up, being bullied at school and misunderstood at home, sometimes we may just feel like giving up.

I try. I try really, really hard. But it seems like, no matter what I do, I just screw it up. Last night, I decided I would help out by making pizza for the family's dinner. I fried up some onions, grated the cheese, drained a can of tomatoes, and put all the toppings on the packaged pizza crust and was ready to put it into the oven, when my dad said, "Did you pre-bake the crust?" I hadn't. So I had to scrape everything off and start over. I feel like I can never get it right.

My parents are always urging me to take more initiative. So one winter morning I got up early to surprise them by cleaning the new snowfall off the cars before they had to go to work. Only, there was so much snow, I decided to use a snow shovel to make the work go faster. Instead of being pleased, they were horrified. I realized too late that, apparently, using a metal snow shovel on a new car is not too good for the paint job. My trying to help cost more than a thousand dollars at the body shop.

It should not come as a surprise that, like everything else we learn early in our lives, learned helplessness begins at home. Every human being begins their life helpless. We cannot change the circumstances of our birth, what kind of parents and siblings we have, what socio-economic group we are born into, what parts of our brain and body will develop when, or whether we will have peace and tranquility at home, or experience the effects of domestic violence, alcoholism, or our parents' divorce. This reality is true for everyone, not just those with NLD.

Like anyone else, we can grasp that certain authority-based rules are the norm ("You have to be at school by 7:45 am," "You are not allowed to drive without a permit"). But while developmentally we are able to comprehend that it is best to obey parents, teachers, and other authorities, often we do not understand *why* these are the rules, and *why* they should apply to us. We want to find out. So we ask questions. And then we ask even more questions. When explanations are not readily forthcoming, or do not make sense, we feel helpless and frustrated.

There are so many questions about NLD and the family for which we simply don't have any answers yet. While there is no denying that the neurological deficits associated with NLD are real, they are not the source of the most difficult challenges for NLDers. Those come from:

- how you are perceived by and treated by others

- how you feel about that and, consequently, how you perceive yourself.

These two factors are iterative. That means that one leads to the other, which feeds on the other, in a kind of never-ending feedback loop. When you are perceived as clumsy, disorganized, and a screw-up, over time you start to think about yourself that way. Then you tend to live up to (or down to) others' expectations of you.

If you treat yourself with respect, others treat you better.

We have looked at many of the ways school officials, therapists, and parents can help us. But much of our success depends upon ourselves. So now what? Are we sunk? Is there any hope? How can we live a successful life with NLD? Read on.

Part IV

Preparing for a Successful Life

Chapter Twelve

Preparing for Academic Success

Special Education classes: help or hindrance?

SPED classes are designed to be helpful. All too often, however, what ends up happening in many school systems is that most SPED students are lumped together into one or more classrooms. Teachers have a finite amount of resources to devote to any one individual student. In most schools, there simply is not the time or staff necessary to provide us with sufficient opportunities to figure out whether or not we even *could* do the work on our own.

In an ideal world, students with dysgraphia would be taught how to write more legibly and more quickly, those with ADD would be taught how to pay better attention, and those with cognitive deficits would end up with average-level IQs. Yet, the reality is that in many, even most, schools, that doesn't actually happen. So, despite the best efforts and intentions of SPED teachers, students still remain dependent on constant assistance from tutors, untimed tests, aides, permission to dictate papers, and so on, at least until we figure out a way out of it all for ourselves, if we are able to do so.

Once in SPED, we usually stay there. Meanwhile, all too often, our "normal" peers tease us, bully us, and make jokes about the "retard class" (in elementary and middle school at least). For all the time the SPED teachers expend trying to stop us "freaks" from being too unruly, not much is spent on teaching us how to be more "normal."

I felt like I was in a strange position. I didn't need help nearly as much as other kids in a SPED class, but I desperately needed the structure and stress-free atmosphere. No matter where I was, I felt I didn't belong.

There really is no definitive answer as to whether or not SPED classes are useful for students with NLD. Like most other facets of living with NLD, it depends. The surveys conducted for this book asked, "Were you at any time during your school career in Special Education (SPED) classes? If so, do you feel that these classes were a help or a hindrance and why?" Here is what we said:

> *No, but I probably should have been there, at least for some classes.*

> *Yes. They were a major help. Nobody made fun of you if you had a resource class.*

> *Yes. They were easier usually.*

> *I think that as good as the intentions might have been of whoever thought up the idea of Special Education in the first place, what it really amounts to is just a dumping ground for any kid who doesn't fit the ideal. They were both a help and a hindrance. They were a help to me because they provided me with accommodations. They were a hindrance to me because I don't think that there was any real effort to have us mainstreamed.*

> *Yes, but only part time—ninth grade and in special speech therapy class. It was a hindrance because I was told to listen instead of read instructions, and I got bored.*

> *They destroyed my self-esteem and did nothing but waste my time.*

> *They were a help because I needed so much help to get through school.*

> *Helpful idea, hindrance in execution—supposedly topics of discussion for the transition period. I have a very hard time with composition, and they required a lot of composition, though the topics themselves were useful.*

> *[SPED class in] elementary school was mostly helpful due to severity of my problems, but also a hindrance due to labeling it the "retard class." Middle school was about the same, but more hindrance. High school was mostly helpful.*

> *A little of both. It helped my stress go down some but the other students sometimes made it worse. I feel like I missed out on some of the better classes.*

Mostly helpful (except for a couple of teachers who shouldn't have had that job at all).

I didn't always feel like I needed them because I had more issues socially than with schoolwork. It only helped me to carve out some time to get some work done, especially in high school. I also didn't feel like I connected much with other kids in that group.

I needed them but the school refused.

I've severe autism… They're helping.

Both helpful and [a] hindrance because many Special Ed teachers are not trained in teaching someone "how to learn" based on the processing challenges prevalent in NLD.

Yes, I quickly learned to read.

IEPs and NLD

In theory at least, the goal of SPED according to the Individuals with Disabilities Education Act (IDEA) is to place the learning disability student in the Least Restrictive Environment (LRE), and if possible, eventually figure out a way to mainstream the student. The Individualized Education Plan (IEP)—a system often thought of as "the heart of IDEA"—is designed to delineate where you are academically, where you should be going, how long it will take to get you there, and how to tell when you have arrived. Or, at least, it is supposed to work that way.

Unfortunately, all too often what happens is that the IEP team — which consists of the LD student, the parents, the SPED teachers, the guidance counselor, and usually a few "regular" teachers—simply takes measure of how screwed up the LD kid is relative to last year.

There is no doubt that the IEP is a complex, perhaps even convoluted, process in which your parents, teachers, principal, and sometimes doctors and therapists convene to determine what services and accommodations are best for the student. Often viewed by the parents and teachers alike as a necessary inconvenience at best, a battleground for fighting for what is "right" at worst, the IEP meeting can often get contentious.

Yet, we often forget that there is more to the contention of IEP meetings than mere lack of understanding legal terminology. What about times when you have one parent in denial that there is anything wrong with you, the other being a helicopter parent (i.e., a parent who constantly hovers over a child, in the sense of being overprotective, overbearing, and over-helping), General Education (GenEd) teachers who demand more services, the SPED teacher claiming he/she is doing all he/she can, and administrators who have nothing to think and nothing to say except, "This isn't working." In times like this, it's best if they would just ask you what accommodations you need. It's just common sense.

Worse still, the way the IEP is worded often sounds much like a CEO writing your New Year's resolutions for you, e.g., "Johnny will improve his gross motor skills by 80 percent." So, what happens if you fall short of 80 percent improvement? It doesn't matter who your teachers are, or what exercise you get at home—it's still worded as though it's your fault, which only serves to indicate how you continue to fall behind and emphasizes your deficits, thereby warranting yet another IEP meeting the following year (and the one after that, and the one after that…).

> No one knew what NLD was. They would not give me an IEP even after being shown the testing results. It would have been great to have an NLD advocate. In high school they thought NLD meant I was struggling with reading (I'm a great reader) so this horrible woman wrote me a detention when I wouldn't take her to the special reading skills center. It was a huge school and I get lost so easily I could barely find my own locker, I had no idea where this place was! That was the end of trying to get accommodations in high school.

The survey asked, "What, in your opinion, could be done to help improve IEPs and IEP meetings for NLDers?" Respondents said:

> For teachers and other staff to take it seriously and make the child feel they're worthy of learning.

> [To have] teacher and staff education in presentation and adaptations and accommodations.

More information to teachers and people who work in education. More emphasis on the importance of education and an educational system that works for all learners.

I personally feel all students, despite having a "disability" should have IEPs and individualized attention when it comes to education, not separate classes.

The meetings should be conducted 1:1, rather than eight people surrounding you, presenting and answering questions from multiple location points in the same room. The anxiety is off the chart. So, the meetings should be in 15-minute blocks with breaks in between.

Let the student give their ideas at the meetings if possible.

Write [the IEP] in clear language.

Probably nothing. It really is just a matter [of] if a teacher wants to work with you or not.

Frequent parent evaluation for IEP.

Stop treating the tests to diagnose like [a] standardized one...figure out individual strengths and run with it.

[Use] visual aids and break it down.

There could be earlier intervention and follow through if such a thing were possible.

Direct involvement with the parents and teachers.

There needs to be a greater understanding. Teachers and educators in general do not know enough about NLD to differentiate fully for students who have it.

One excellent resource for NLDers and their parents is the 2014 book *Parents Have the Power to Make Special Education Work*, by Judith Canty Graves and Carson Graves,[73] and its website.[74]

Ultimately, we need to redesign both the IEP itself and the IEP meeting process so that they are much more student friendly. One alternate model that I found helpful is the Jewish Educational Action Plan (JEAP), an IEP for Hebrew schools, designed by Sandy Miller-Jacobs for the Bureau of Jewish Education of Greater Boston (BJE).[75]

If we remove the Judaism-specific material, we find that the main differences between the JEAP and the IEP are that the JEAP is voluntary and gathers information from the parents and children themselves in a respectful manner, going so far as to ask, "What motivates the child?", "What are the student's interests?", and "What situations are difficult?" The IEP does not seem to take any of these into consideration. If only it did, we might end up with a SPED system that actually worked to help you overcome your symptoms, or, at the very least, not have the same objective— "3.2.5: [Name] will improve his handwriting in four out of five instances"—that first was posited in the IEP in the first grade remain until the student's senior year.

For all the help that SPED classes and our teachers and aides are supposed to be giving us, sometimes—maybe a lot of the time— when it comes to succeeding in school, we just have to figure out for ourselves what works and what doesn't. To help you, those who were interviewed and surveyed for this book shared many of the techniques that helped them. Maybe you will find one or more of these tips useful for you.

Study skills

There seem to be three ways people with NLD can study effectively. The first is *auditory memorization,* or learning from listening or from reading aloud:

> *I read the material out loud into a tape recorder and then listen to it in order to review for tests, etc.*

> *I read my notes into a tape recorder and then listened to them over and over again. If any teachers gave us essay questions in advance, I made sure to answer them and then memorize my answer.*

The second technique is *visual memorization,* or reading what you are studying:

> *Read over my notes, read the relevant material, looking for alternative explanations of the material online. I prefer to read whenever possible, as I hate making "flashcards."*

Reviewing the notes for all tests except math. In math I did lots of practice problems.

Simply reading over the material. As my organizational skills are poor, I never developed any complex study skills. The more I am interested in the material, the more I will soak it up. If I am not interested or if there is a heavy emphasis on visual material, the motivation is simply not there but I do what I have to do to pass.

Using flashcards, using color-coded pens to write (e.g. using a different color for headings, different color for vocabulary words).

Flashcards were extremely useful for studying vocab, both for foreign language classes and for the SATs. Also in terms of reviewing for a final, using the Outline mode in Microsoft Word. That way, you can organize your notes into categories, subcategories, etc. Reading straight through the textbook has only worked for me in history classes.

We also used *group study and/or a combination of the other* techniques:

Groups, where studying was done casually.

Being quizzed through auditory memory by someone else, memorization, discussion with classmates.

Making an outline of what to study—being able to talk over the subject aloud with someone—reading the textbooks/notes aloud—having someone quiz me verbally, and prompting me for things I forget—making mnemonics and songs about information.

Reading aloud, writing summaries and telling others what I learned (even my imaginary friends).

Writing notes, and then returning to my room to type on the computer, reviewing three times, and studying with partners sometimes.

Note-taking

We may write so slowly that note-taking is physically difficult or impossible, or we may have trouble both writing and listening at the same time:

I don't take notes, both because I write incredibly slowly, and also because if I focus too much on writing, I can't focus on what is being taught. So

I only write something down if it's a definition or something I can't get elsewhere, something visual like a flowchart.

Or, we may write fast enough, but have difficulty being able to pick out the salient points:

I try, but almost never take notes worth looking at again.

Yes. I write fast, and just write everything down that I can. (A friend used to say, "When the teacher tells us to take out our notebooks, you take yours out and write 'take out your notebooks'!" ;-))

I wrote EVERYTHING down and I kept the notes per subject in one single folder.

Yes, I did take notes, but I never learned a good system or went back to study them much.

I do take notes, although I tend to write down much more than I needed. Never have gotten a great system—I never know what information is important and what is not. Oh well, grad school is over in two months anyway.

This respondent summed up both challenges very well:

No, never. I could not write fast enough, and even if I could, I could not write and pay attention at the same time. I could never figure out which things the teacher was saying were most important.

So what do we do? Some of us *use technology* to help us:

I have an AlphaSmart. In high school when I had access to a laptop but didn't want to bring it to class, I seldom wrote any notes. I have developed the ability to be a quick and efficient typist and I can take very thorough notes with my AlphaSmart. I find carrying a laptop around and having to plug it in to be too much of a hassle and that is why an AlphaSmart is ideal.

Keeping all notes electronically is downright mandatory, as I'm unable to organize papers easily. With all of my notes stored on Google Docs, I simply search for the topic I need, and the information is readily available from anywhere.

Or we call on *our friends* or *an aide:*

No. I can't keep up if I do. I mooch off my friends' notes, they're usually pretty cool about running off photocopies.

I tried, but I could not write fast enough. Instead I would underline or highlight parts of the texts, or borrow notes from a friend.

In high school, I found it very hard to write while the teacher was talking. The teacher always spoke fast, and by the time I interpreted it and wrote it down, the teacher was already way ahead. In college, I qualify for note-takers. This facilitates things since I can read the text to prepare and then just listen in class.

We may draw upon a combination of *other people and technology*:

Memorizing every word that is spoken and asking people what this means then memorizing that with the original speech. Could never write well enough to take notes, tape recorder worked well but the background noise made it impossible to listen to. Laptop computer would have worked and is my new plan.

Some of us ask our *teachers* to structure lectures to match our needs:

Yes, and the system that works best is if the teacher has notes available to look at while lecturing and to take home for me to type up on the computer.

So while note-taking may continue to be a challenge for those of us with NLD, you can try using technology, asking your teacher to provide a lesson outline, asking friends for help, or requesting an aide.

Organizing longer assignments and papers

One respondent describes the difference *good teaching* can make:

All the way through high school, when I was given an assignment, I would just sit and stare at the blank page, hoping and waiting for inspiration to strike. If it didn't, I just would be paralyzed. I knew I couldn't write a paper. It never occurred to me that other people had trouble too, that they did bad first drafts. I thought everyone else just had great ideas, and they could write starting from Point A to Point Z, writing a perfect paper on the first try. No one thought to tell me that this was not true. If I couldn't write perfectly on the first try, I would just shut down and not do the assignment at all. I got a lot of "zeros" and flunked every single English course in high school for that reason. I finally learned in college freshman English how to write a paper. Pick a topic, express it in one or two sentences. Then write down about four to six thoughts that support that topic. Then make an outline, then write. My freshman English teacher required us to turn in every step along the way so we couldn't skip any. Topic sentence—turn it in. Supporting ideas—turn them in. Paragraphs, first draft, revisions—she looked at every step. I started getting As on every paper using this method. Learning this technique completely improved my academic performance in all subjects, not to mention my self-esteem.

In addition to being lucky enough to have effective teachers, we have figured out methods that work for us.

My writing skills are very poor. My spoken voice is much better; therefore I plan to use voice transcribing software when I continue my education.

Some of us use a "scatter-shot" method that involves writing down one idea, then another idea, and so on, and then trying to use a transition sentence to make all these disparate ideas flow into the main idea. This is probably the least effective method of getting a paper done. Because many people with NLD also tend to be perfectionists, it can take a *really* long time to get a paper done using this method.

When I have a paper assigned, I try to allow myself one full day to produce a page of writing.

I usually talk about it out loud (either to myself or someone else). I usually also need a day or two off. And a lot of times, I need to read a lot (of anything) first.

I start writing whatever comes to mind, then I revise multiple times by inserting the necessary information and correcting the grammar and structure.

Before I write a paper, I give myself a vague idea of what my arguments will be and then I start writing. I never have made outlines with any degree of detail. This system has allowed for me to get Bs for the most part. I think my difficulty with organizing and my tendency to stray from the initial essay question has prevented me from excelling beyond that.

Some of us use either low-tech methods or more advanced *technology* to help us with our writing:

I write all the facts on index cards, then I categorize the cards and make piles. From there, I start writing.

I begin by making a short informal list of topics I need to cover, and the order I should cover them in. Then, I use a distraction-free word processor called Dark Room to freewrite my thoughts, going through multiple iterations of the same section or idea. After I develop a basic idea of how the essay should look, I paste the text into Microsoft Word and organize from there.

My computer is my best friend. I can't put it much better than that.

Or we may use a technique called *mind mapping*, a particular form of brainstorming. It is basically a kind of flowchart, in which you write down ideas on one topic, then on others, and then using lines and arrows, you make connections between and among ideas that have a causal link.

First, I brainstorm and write down every word that comes up. Then I write down the structure of the paper: section one = introduction, section two = etc. Then I start writing.

In college I knew it would take me a LOT longer to write papers so I allowed a lot of extra time. I finally figured out a system of making a graph or chart of what I was writing about, then what points supported the main point, then details and quotes from other sources.

Dumping and then having someone edit to make sure that it sounds correct, spider diagrams helped to get ideas out and organized by topic. Started in the middle and then went back to the beginning to write a thesis statement.

One good book that talks about mind mapping is *Learning Outside the Lines: Two Ivy League Students with Learning Disabilities and ADHD Give You The Tools.*[76] Written by Jonathan Mooney and David Cole, who, as the title suggests, speak from experience about what it is like to attend college when you have a learning disability, it gives lots of practical tips about study skills, note-taking, and life away from home. And the book is extremely well-organized, making it easy to use.

Outlining consists of making a list of topics you want to cover, then listing subtopics under each general topic, then writing proofs for each subtopic.

> *I pour all my thoughts out, and then systematically organize my papers. I have done very well in English, excelling in essays.*

> *Introduction—point 1—subpoints—point 2—subpoints—point 3, 4, conclusion.*

> *First, come up with a thesis. Then come up with three to five points to support the thesis. Then three to five subpoints for each of those. And then for each of the subpoints, make sure you have supporting quotes or data. Then the rest is just adding transition sentences to connect the main thoughts to one another. Then, write the conclusion and then write the abstract if one is needed. Then I make sure that I have it edited for me, first for content, then I write the next draft, then have it edited and proofread.*

> *I have a system, but I can't describe it, it's too hard. It was taught to me. It involves writing down each category, Introduction, Part I, then in each category breaking it down further, i.e., a, b, c, d, and into i, ii, iii, iv, etc.*

Sometimes, we may have trouble staying motivated enough to finish a long assignment. If our parents are willing to provide the rewards, some also find it useful and fun to build in a reward system for each step or for finishing a project. If not, we can create our own rewards, such as taking a break, buying a pizza, going for a walk, watching a movie, or listening to favorite music. Following are several worksheets developed by my mother, Gail Shapiro, a Professional Organizer.[77]

WORKSHEET 1: STEPS TO ORGANIZING A RESEARCH OR ESSAY PAPER

1. **Get assignment** (from class syllabus or when it's given).

2. Immediately **read the entire assignment** for clarity. If you have any questions, ask the teacher/professor.

3. Figure out the exact **steps you will need** to take in order to complete the assignment correctly and on time, using this model as a template.

4. **Calculate** approximately how long each of the steps will take.

5. **Schedule** each step and the time allowed into your master calendar. Allow **five hours** of writing time to produce a good draft of one page, exclusive of research and planning time.

Repeat Steps 1 through 5 for each assignment you now have in hand (even ones that are due after this assignment, because you will probably be doing early steps of later assignments at the same time you are completing an earlier assignment). Now, back to the first paper due.

6. **Choose a topic** (if it is an essay), or **find and read** the book or books (if it is an analysis). Is it a novel or popular book that you can get **on CD (or Playaway or MP3)**?

7. Find and read the **primary sources** (if it is a research paper).

8. If necessary, get the topic **approved** by teacher/professor.

9. Look at the assignment again. If there is a choice of questions, **choose one question**.

10. **Create your thesis** and write it in one sentence.

11. Write **3–5 sentences** (depending on length of final paper) that support your thesis.

12. From library or the internet, **find secondary sources**. How many will you need? Which are most appropriate?

13. Look through or **read secondary sources**, marking good quotes with a highlighter or sticky notes.

14. Begin to **write the draft**. From this point on, plan on needing **five hours** to produce **one page** of writing.

15. **Reread the assignment**. Be sure you are answering the question completely and thoroughly.

16. When draft is finished, you can **send it out to an aide or tutor** for an edit/proof.

17. **Make edits** and any changes.

18. Create a **bibliography** or works-cited page.

19. Create any **handouts,** visuals, illustrations, charts, notes for oral presentation, etc. that may be required.

20. Produce a **final draft** and turn it in early or on time.

21. **Pat yourself** on the back. Get a reward or treat!

22. Get busy on the **next paper** or project.

WORKSHEET 2: ORGANIZING AN ESSAY OR RESEARCH PAPER (WITH REWARDS AND CHECKLIST)

1. **Get assignment** (from class syllabus or when given). Read all the syllabi on the first day of each class and put a check mark next to each writing assignment.

    How long will this take?_____ Due date for this step:_____

    When will I do this step?_____ Reward points:_____

    Completed ☐

2. Immediately **read the entire assignment** for clarity. If you have questions, ask the professor.

    How long will this take?_____ Due date for this step:_____

    When will I do this step?_____ Reward points:_____

    Completed ☐

3. Figure out the exact **steps you will need** to take in order to complete the assignment correctly and on time, using this model as a template.

    How long will this take?_____ Due date for this step:_____

    When will I do this step?_____ Reward points:_____

    Completed ☐

4. **Calculate** approximately how long each of the steps will take.

    How long will this take?_____ Due date for this step:_____

    When will I do this step?_____ Reward points:_____

    Completed ☐

5. **Schedule** each step and write down the time allowed into your master calendar. Allow **five hours** of writing time to produce a good draft of one page, excluding research and planning time.

    How long will this take?_____ Due date for this step:_____

    When will I do this step?_____ Reward points:_____

    Completed ☐

Repeat Steps 1 through 5 for each assignment you now have in hand (even ones that are due after this assignment, because you will probably be doing early steps of later assignments at the same time you are completing an earlier assignment).

6. Now, back to the first paper due.

    a.   **Choose a topic** (if an essay).

       How long will this take?_____ Due date for this step:_____

       When will I do this step?_____ Reward points:_____

       Completed ☐

    b.   And/or **find the book** (if a report).

       How long will this take?_____ Due date for this step:_____

       When will I do this step?_____ Reward points:_____

       Completed ☐

    c.   **Read** the book or books (if an analysis). Is it a novel or popular book that you can get **on CD, Playaway, or MP3**? If so, ask the library to get it for you.

       How long will this take?_____ Due date for this step:_____

       When will I do this step?_____ Reward points:_____

       Completed ☐

7. Find and read the **primary sources** (if research).

   How long will this take?_____ Due date for this step:_____

   When will I do this step?_____ Reward points:_____

   Completed ☐

8. If necessary, get your topic **approved** by the teacher or professor.

   How long will this take?_____ Due date for this step:_____

   When will I do this step?_____ Reward points:_____

   Completed ☐

9. Look at the assignment again. If there is a choice of questions, **choose one question**.

   How long will this take?_____ Due date for this step:_____

   When will I do this step?_____ Reward points:_____

   Completed ☐

10. **Create your thesis** and write it in one sentence.

   How long will this take?_____ Due date for this step:_____

   When will I do this step?_____ Reward points:_____

   Completed ☐

11. Write **3–5 sentences** (depending on the length of the final paper) that support your thesis.

How long will this take?_____ Due date for this step:_____

When will I do this step?_____ Reward points:_____

Completed ☐

12. From library or the internet, **find secondary sources**. How many will you need? Which are most appropriate?

How long will this take?_____ Due date for this step:_____

When will I do this step?_____ Reward points:_____

Completed ☐

13. Look through or **read secondary sources**, marking good quotes with a highlighter or sticky notes.

How long will this take?_____ Due date for this step:_____

When will I do this step?_____ Reward points:_____

Completed ☐

14. Begin to **write the draft**. From this point on, plan on needing **five hours** to produce **one page** of writing.

How long will this take?_____ Due date for this step:_____

When will I do this step?_____ Reward points:_____

Completed ☐

15. **Reread the assignment**. *This is critical!* Be sure you are answering the question completely and thoroughly.

How long will this take?_____ Due date for this step:_____

When will I do this step?_____ Reward points:_____

Completed ☐

16. When the draft is finished, you can **send it to your aide or tutor** for an edit/proof.

How long will this take?_____ Due date for this step:_____

When will I do this step?_____ Reward points:_____

Completed ☐

17. **Make edits** and changes.

How long will this take?_____ Due date for this step:_____

When will I do this step?_____ Reward points:_____

Completed ☐

18. Create a **bibliography** or works-cited page.

    How long will this take?_____ Due date for this step:_____

    When will I do this step?_____ Reward points:_____

    Completed ☐

19. Create any **handouts,** visuals, illustrations, charts, notes for oral presentation, etc. that may be required.

    How long will this take?_____ Due date for this step:_____

    When will I do this step?_____ Reward points:_____

    Completed ☐

20. Produce a **final draft** and turn it in early or on time.

    How long will this take?_____ Due date for this step:_____

    When will I do this step?_____ Reward points:_____

    Completed ☐

21. Pat yourself on the back. **Get a reward** or treat!

    How long will this take?_____ Due date for this step:_____

    When will I do this step?_____ Reward points:_____

    Completed ☐

22. Get busy on the **next paper** or project.

WORKSHEET 3: SUPER REWARD
CHART FOR BOOK REPORTS

(Note: *Hamlet* is used here as an example of an assigned reading. Adapt this sample chart by filling in your own assignments and your own rewards!)

Rewards for completing steps in writing analysis of *Hamlet*

This task	If completed by this time	# prize points
1. Annotated bibliography	**9:00 pm**, November 12	15 points
2. *Hamlet* Thesis plus 3–5 supporting sentences plus secondary source quotes marked with sticky notes plus one page of first draft	**Noon**, November 13	20 points
3. *Hamlet* pages 2-4 of first draft	**9:00 pm**, November 13	25 points
4. *Hamlet* page 5 of first draft	**10:00 am**, November 14	10 points
5. *Hamlet* page 6 of first draft	**4:00 pm**, November 14	10 points
6. *Hamlet* Completed first draft, submit to aide for edits	**3:00 pm**, November 16	40 points
7. *Hamlet*, works-cited page	**3:00 pm**, November 17	5 points

Rules: Task must be done in full, by time specified. **No partial points** for partial task completion. All prize points must be redeemed by November 21.

Rewards redemption chart

Lunch at a restaurant of your choice	35 points
"Get out of weekly chores free" card	45 points
One Scrabble game	10 points
Trip to bowling alley	100 points
Movie of your choice in theater	50 points
Watch a DVD of your choice	15 points
Order in take-out food	40 points
$20 credit at bookstore or music store	50 points

Time management

Time Management is really tough. I've even read books to try to improve, but they all seem to be written for people without NLD.

There are many organizing books on the market that can help you with time management skills, but not many are suitable for those with NLD. In addition, most of us really resent having people tell us we need to "get organized." "Getting organized" seems like just one more opportunity for frustration. But if you can get over the resentment, being organized—up to a point—really does save time and energy. Some really helpful books I've encountered are: Julie Morgenstern's *Time Management from the Inside Out*[78] and *Organizing from the Inside Out,*[79] as well as Peter Walsh's *How to Organize (Just About) Everything.*[80] If you need one-on-one help, you can hire a Professional Organizer to work with you. To find one near you, and as for a general aide to figure out what you might need help with, visit the website of the National Association of Professional Organizers (NAPO).[81]

Because right now going to school is your primary job, the skills discussed here have to do with organizing school-based projects. Some of the tips can be adapted to life at work, and all can be used for life at college.

Our respondents shared tips for using *planning tools*:

I write important dates and deadlines on a calendar that's clearly visible that I can't miss, so that way I don't usually [miss]!

I use my alarm a lot if I can't work on something longer than a certain time. When the alarm goes, I need to stop doing what I'm doing, no matter whether it is finished or not. Over time, I learned to check how much time I have left and I get sidetracked less. Still, I very often don't accomplish the goal in the time set.

This hasn't been a huge problem for me. I just make a list every day of what I have to accomplish, and also what is coming up in the future. The main problem is what things come up during the day that are NOT on the list. They tend to throw me off track.

I use Google Calendar to remember important dates and events, and I use Remember The Milk to show tasks and due dates. Both show as modules on my Google homepage, so I'm constantly reminded of what I have to do. They're also both accessible from my phone, so I can add an event or task before I have the opportunity to forget it.

After YEARS of resistance, I finally got a calendar. I now write down all appointments, meetings, etc. when I make them, and then remember to look at the calendar every morning when I have my coffee. That way I don't forget places I have to go or people I have to call. I also write down long-term things, like "go see the dentist" six months ahead so I remember to make the appointment in a timely way. This has helped a lot. I wish I hadn't been such a stubborn fool for so long. It was because I am an artist and musician—and we creative types don't need to be bound by ordinary rules. Well, that would be fine if the rest of the world worked on artist-time, but after getting bounced from a couple of jobs and losing a couple of friends, I finally figured it out.

Some of us ask for *help or accommodations:*

I have a planner. I meet with an LD coach once a week.

Taking a lighter course load. Right now I am taking 60 percent of a full course load. This way, I am under MUCH less stress. Having to take at least one and likely two extra years [to finish college] is well worth being able to actually enjoy the courses that are of interest to me without being under the constant stress that even my non-NLD peers who take a full course load are under.

We *keep our lives simple:*

[Don't really have a system.] I make very few commitments, to avoid this one altogether.

Do the work. Forget there is such a thing called a social life.

And *sticking to a routine* really helps:

When I was in school it was best if I did my homework right after school. I also did harder assignments (like math) first, because I had more energy and also to get them out of the way.

Yes, once a routine is established, I do well.

Well, people ask how I can do grad. school, my thesis, work four jobs and remember to live. I say it really helps to have no social life and no friends—which is true. You'd be amazed how much time people waste on friends (sarcastic). I make sure I get enough sleep, always, which helps, and I block out chunks for studying and chunks of break time, because if I don't take breaks when I should, I'll end up taking them when I have to or messing up at a job or something.

Project management

Keeping track of multiple projects and assignments in school, plus routine chores at home, doctor and dentist appointments, and meetings with friends, sometimes it's tough to remember everything.

Here is a system you may find helpful:

1. **List** all the things you have to do or want to do, both current and in the near future, into one big list.

2. **Sort** by priority: What has to be done right now or today? What has to be done tomorrow or the day after that? Are there deadlines attached to any of the other items? If so, what are they? Working backwards from each deadline, what are the steps necessary to make them happen on time?

or

3. **Sort** by project: For example, English paper on *Hamlet*, volunteer to help make Spanish club posters, making holiday cards for relatives and friends. Are there deadlines attached to any of these items? If so, what are they? Working backwards from each deadline, what are the steps necessary to make them happen on time?

4. **Decide:** which items can be delegated or eliminated for now. Delegate or eliminate.

5. **Transfer:** items onto your daily to-do list or onto your running to-do list. Add deadlines if applicable.

6. **Start doing** items: When finished, check off. Transfer any undone daily to-do items to the next day's list. Keep working on your running list, moving things to the daily list as needed per deadlines.

Every day I divide what needs to be done into the following categories: "Must do," "Should do," "Want to do," and "Coming up." Then from the

"Must do" list, I select one or two "Most important goals" for the day, and make sure I get to those first.

You also might try keeping a weekly chart of projects and write down when each is due. Here is an example:

To do week of:

When due:
Steps to complete:
Finish:
Homework:
Papers/tests:
Meetings/appointments:
Calls/letters/emails:
Job/other obligations:

If you have trouble keeping track of what you have to do every day, there are several different apps for your smart phone. Because apps and software programs come and go, you can visit my website,[82] to see what other NLDers find useful, and to suggest your own favorites.

Or for the low-tech version, you can try a simple daily "to-do" list. When you list on paper or on your phone or computer all the things you have to do, they no longer clutter up your brain. The trick is to remember to make the list every night before bed, and then to look at it every morning. Pick no more than three "most important goals" for the day, then list the others in their order of importance. When you check off an item, you get a feeling of accomplishment! Here is one example of an organizing template:

TO DO: NOVEMBER 18

Most important goals

- Take a walk for 45 minutes.
- Turn in Hamlet paper.
- Call Grandma to wish her a happy birthday.

Must do

- Eat breakfast.
- Take a shower and get dressed.
- Go to school.
- Answer emails.
- Finish homework.
- My turn to cook dinner tonight.

Should do

- Help fix Mom's computer.
- Do a load of laundry.
- Get hair cut this afternoon.
- Start on the math assignment due next week.

Would like to do

- Take a nap.
- Watch The Simpsons at 7:30 pm.

Next day/coming up

- Start looking for a book for next book report.

With these tips and others that you may use yourself, you are going to become a lot better at succeeding in school. But how do you succeed in your relationships? Read on.

Chapter Thirteen

NLD, Friendships, and Dating

I didn't know what was socially appropriate for the longest time, so people would think I was weird and stay away from me. I'm now just starting to learn what is socially appropriate. My parents used to get mad at me. I didn't understand why. I still don't understand why people get mad at me when I'm just trying my best to please people.

Everyone wants to have friends—one or more people you can trust, count on, share good times with—people who are there for you through good times and bad times. NLDers are no different. Some—but not all of us—also might want to have a love interest, either now or in the future.

How do you find someone to be your friend or partner?

The answer to this question is the subject of so many songs, not to mention magazine articles, websites, and blogs, and there are even whole books about making friends and developing social skills, so it doesn't make sense to repeat all that information here.

In interviewing the subjects and conducting the surveys for this edition, there is plenty of evidence that many—though not all—NLDers may be introverts. Introverts are often happiest with a few, deep friendships. Even one or two friendships can be enough. If this sounds like you, it's important to stop judging yourself against a world run by extroverts and know that—no matter what your parents, siblings, or teachers think—it's perfectly OK to have just one or two good friends. (Although the original 1967 guess made by Isabel Myers of the Myers-Briggs test was that the division was about 25% to 75%, introverts to extroverts, more recent research, from 1998 on, shows that based on people who actually took the test, the actual ratio is very close to 50% each.)[83]

As to how to make and keep friends, here are our best suggestions.

Look outside your peer group for friendships
Go up or down a generation or cohort

NLDers often get along great with small kids and with adults—because small kids don't judge and older folks have the maturity to be patient with our long-winded talking and "odd" mannerisms.

Consider volunteering at an old folks' home. Go to your local Council on Aging or Senior Center in your town, and play Scrabble or bridge with the seniors. Listen to their stories. You will get the benefit of their wisdom and hear their stories and listen to the hardships they've overcome and you won't feel so alone or isolated. Plus, in a very few years, you will be an adult, so this won't be so weird.

If you're in high school especially, getting along with friends too often is going along with a slew of fart jokes.

So much about life in high school revolves around "fitting in." Teens often are afraid to be different from their peers. Don't be. NLDers already are so "different," not only from other SPED kids, but from their neurotypical classmates, that it hardly matters. Just be yourself and you'll do fine—eventually.

Understand that NO relationship is ever "perfect"

Many NLDers think that if they can't "do it right" when it comes to friendships, they can't do it at all. Everyone makes mistakes. Everyone screws up sometimes. And when you care for someone, it is likely that, at some point, you will hurt them or they will hurt you. What's important to note is the intention: did they mean to hurt you? Did you set out deliberately to hurt them? If not, the friendship can usually be repaired.

I can count on one hand the number of friends who will stick with me through thick and thin, and they really, really matter to me.

Find people who share your interests

The way you make friends is—whatever the "experts" on NLD or other learning disabilities may say about having social skills deficits, or any other nomenclature to that effect—if you meet someone who shares your same interests, ideas, values, political or religious views, or taste in music or books, then you may have found the basis for a friendship. You may disagree with them at times, maybe even a lot of the time, but if you share interests or ideas together, you keep talking.

> *I've found making friends in the mental health community to be very helpful.*

Be the kind of person you'd like to have for a friend

Are you the kind of person you would want to be friends with? As a start, first you have to be a good friend to yourself. This may be a radical idea for you. What does it mean?

> *You don't talk to yourself in mean or negative ways. You don't "beat yourself up" if you think you did something wrong.*

> *Start viewing yourself as a valuable person with something to offer.*

What are some of the qualities you think make a good friend? Other NLDers have said:

> *Someone who is smart and really interesting.*

> *Someone who is loyal, kind, and funny.*

> *My friends may be quirky, but they get me.*

> *I really appreciate someone who is a good listener, and who is not afraid to be vulnerable.*

> *To develop healthy friendships, you actually have to like yourself. Be the very best person you can be, and you will be a good friend. This can be very difficult when you've experienced learned helplessness, when you've been used, abused, and so confused for much of your school life.*

> *I really was not so much into the hair/nails/makeup/boys/fashion thing. I actually was more interested in professional football. So for a long time, most of my friends were guys, not other girls.*

> *You need to pursue your OWN interests—even if those aren't the "cool" or "popular" things to do at your school. Even if that makes you "weird"*

or "different" you can be sure someone else somewhere also is interested in the same thing.

When you have NLD, you have many characteristics that potentially make you very successful in relationships. Why do NLDers make great friends or partners?

We won't lie to you, and we won't betray you. One, because we tend to value the truth very highly; two, because we know we are very lucky to have you, and aren't willing to risk screwing it up by our own actions.

The flip side of that is: we WILL tell you the truth—the whole truth. If you ask, "Does this dress make me look fat?" we are likely to say, "Yeah. So what? Move on."

We will definitely respect your need and right to be alone sometimes. We are not clingy. You want "me time?" Guess what? We do too.

We are really great at keeping a secret. The thing is, though, first you need to say explicitly, "This is a secret." Then we're fine.

We have very little tolerance for B.S. and drama. We get enough of that elsewhere.

We are REALLY happy to talk to you—any old time you want.

And we are really good listeners too. We've learned to be sensitive to others' pain—we've had a lot of our own to deal with.

Loyalty. We are very, very loyal. If we are your friend or partner, we will always have your back.

Spend some time learning to develop the basic social skills that others expect

Let's start with the basics. Everybody should practice good hygiene, including taking a shower or bath every day, having one's hair cut regularly and a neat hairstyle, shaving daily, having clean and trimmed nails, and having clean and pressed (or at least not wrinkled and torn) clothing. If you wear leather shoes, they should be polished; if not, shoes should at least be clean.

If you wear makeup, remember that it's designed to enhance your appearance, not hide it. Be aware that not everyone may share your enthusiasm for facial piercings, and consider removing them when appropriate, for example at your house of worship or at a job interview.

Because some NLDers have sensory sensitivity issues, we like to wear our old, comfy clothes—sometimes even if they have holes in them. That's fine for hanging around the house or with your friends, if they also dress casually. But for "public appearances," like school, religious services, doctor visits, airplane travel, and going out with your parents, you should plan to look appropriate.

As far as style, guys can check out Esquire Magazine's *The Handbook of Style: A Man's Guide to Looking Good*.[84] It covers just about all rules imaginable about clothes, from jeans to suits, haircuts to shoes, and everything in between. And it gives a really clear reason for every fashion rule, important for NLDers. Plus it's really funny. Strangely, I haven't found any similar books for women, so if you know of any, please let me know.

If your parents are always after you to improve your table manners, try to understand that they are not trying to be mean or controlling, rather, they are trying to prepare you for the outside world, where it is not considered polite to make slurping noises with your soup, or to have your elbows on the table.

Why is it important to have good table manners? Well for one thing, it's hard to know what you look like eating unless you do it in front of a mirror. And when you gobble food, eat with your fingers, and eat the way you might do when you are alone, it looks kind of gross to others. Plus, your parents worry that if you have to eat in public, like at a restaurant or job interview, you won't know how to do it politely.

It is helpful to learn the rules of etiquette, which are important to a lot of people, including the people who might hire you, admit you into their college, or pay your bills. Then you have the option to "be correct" when you want to.

When you say the word "etiquette," many people think of Emily Post. Though she is long gone, her great-granddaughter-in-law Peggy Post has continued her work and produced a number of very good, informative books on the subject. One of these, co-written with Emily Post's great-granddaughter Cindy Post Senning and Sharon Watts, is *Teen Manners: From Malls to Meals to Messaging and*

Beyond.[85] It covers just about everything else you need to know about manners, and more importantly for NLDers: why you need to know this stuff. The Emily Post Institute also has a website called Teen Manners,[86] which gives excerpts from the book.

Another website called RudeBusters![87] billing itself as "A safe haven from rudeness, rage and stress" has much useful information presented in an easy-to-understand manner.

Because we may have trouble finding out how to read and interpret social cues, most NLDers need actual step-by-step clarification and instruction. One good book, addressed to teens through adults is, *Will I Ever Fit In?: The Breakthrough Program for Conquering Adult Dyssemia* by Stephen Nowicki and Marshall P. Duke.[88]

This book is very useful, in that it not only explains, but also shows you how to improve, all aspects of nonverbal communication: gaze and eye contact, body space and touch, paralanguage (tone, loudness, and pace of speech), facial expression, gestures and postures, fashion and hygiene, social rules and norms, nonverbal receptivity, conversational skills, and timing and rhythm.

In the survey and interviews, NLDers were asked, "Have you found helpful strategies to find and keep friends?" We said:

> *Sometimes just keep quiet when you don't quite understand another person, take your time to formulate sensitive questions, be careful to associate with people who seem to be more open minded and with a more generous heart.*

> *I have one friend. Part of the problem is that I lose my patience with people who are close to me and then they get angry and move on.*

> *Keeping the expectations to a minimum that others might have on me is always a challenge. I always need to be in familiar environments if there are expectations of me.*

> *I don't find that my NLD has any effect on my relationships.*

> *It's NOT a crime to be an introvert, you know! That said, make sure you have one or two BFFs who you will always be there for and who will always be there for you.*

> *Oh, yes. Listen a LOT MORE than talk. I lost a LOT of friends when I was younger because I couldn't keep my opinions to myself and kept*

right on talking, ignoring all social cues. I'm a lot better at that now, but definitely not perfect.

Don't wait for others to call you. AND, if your friends tell you they have other plans, that could be exactly what it means: they have other plans. NOT, oh my lord they don't like me, etc.

I withdraw socially sometimes when I am overwhelmed and that makes it hard to maintain friendships. Sometimes I won't want to meet you places because I am anxious about how to get there. Sometimes people think I am being careless when I bump into things or write something down and it's not very neat.

Yes, there have been far too many points in my life, especially in high school and college, when I came off as a totally naïve ass.

Some of the *resources* we've found useful are:

I study body language, I network online with other people who have NLD.

Meetups and groups.

Therapy groups, Facebook, meetups and books.

Yes, a Yahoo NLD group for adults.

Our pastor has been really helpful. (I sort of suspect he may have NLD too but he might just be really empathetic.) I used to belong to a couple of online groups but they seem to have disappeared.

Practicing mindfulness, most often.

When you are ready to date

Whether a boyfriend/girlfriend, or an eventual life partner or spouse, the rules for romantic relationships are pretty much the same as for making friends. Just as in a friendship, you first have to have a successful relationship with yourself. That way, you will be the best possible partner for someone else.

In the most recent survey, in answer to the question, "Which of the following best describes your current relationship status?" 57.14 percent of respondents said, "single, never married," 14.29 percent said, "single, cohabiting with a significant other," 21.43

percent are married, and 7.14 percent are divorced. The survey also asked for tips and experiences in navigating relationships, and whether this was difficult. Many respondents simply said, "Yes," while others elaborated:

> *I haven't had a [romantic] relationship yet, I am too nervous about not being able to understand the other person's needs or attempts at communication, I am too nervous to believe that I am good enough for a relationship with my communication deficits.*

> *Well, I think my husband has NLD too, maybe Asperger's, but he doesn't have a diagnosis. We just have to talk things out a lot, so yes, more challenging, but not impossible. We get along pretty well most of the time.*

> *Yes, but I am dating again. It's hard but worth it.*

> *I've had one boyfriend and we've been together for 14+ years. We're both neurodiverse, so that helps. Give your partner space when they need it and tell them when you need space.*

> *I have avoided romance, and I'm just not really interested in it just yet. I was slower to mature than my typical peers.*

> *Don't be overbearing even though we're looking for constant reassurance and approval. Don't ever try to be something you are not as a defensive distraction. The NLDer (me) who sees you across the room knows it's bullshit, and loves you all the more for you just being you.*

> *Always listen.*

Because NLDers tend to be very trusting and sometimes naïve, when you feel ready socially and emotionally for a romantic relationship, it's a good idea to read up on the difference between healthy and unhealthy relationships.

> *I am often generous to a fault and easily taken advantage of.*

> *My first boyfriend was very controlling. He wanted to know where I was all the time, and then he tried to tell me who I could be friends with, what I should wear, and stuff like that. It made me very uncomfortable, and I found out much later—after I dumped his sorry self—that those*

were some of the first warning signs for an abusive relationship. So I got out in time, whew!

I really liked my ex-girlfriend, but it seems all she was ever interested in was where I could take her and what I would buy for her.

I have dated some but most of the guys were immature and possessive.

If, like many of us, you are now in high school and have never been on a date, what to do and how to start dating may seem totally overwhelming.

The whole dating scene can be very scary and frustrating for NLDers. Having trouble reading social cues can backfire in any number of ways. We may miss both jokes and actual overtures from possible dating partners, and far beyond the average biological period of latency, we may not even understand why others think sexual activity is pleasurable. And even if we are successful at getting a date, we may get dumped on early because we either come on too strong or because we act "clingy."

> *I only dated once in high school, and that was for the prom. After trying to find someone—anyone—who would go with me, I finally went with one of the relatively geeky girls from the class above me. I thought she was a love interest. I tried to give her a present on Valentine's Day. I gave her this whole basket of Lindt chocolate truffles. And instead of returning any kind of favor—I mean, I didn't really expect to get kissed, but I thought she might at least give me a card or something—instead, she just answered me by giving me one of those hugs that says, "Oh, don't worry, you'll get it right someday." Yeah, right, kind of one of those brush-offs. It was not even a "let's-be-friends" hug. It was more, "you are a total freakin' idiot when it comes to this love thing, so OK, I wish you well, but in the meantime, 'wouldn't you know it, I've got to go to second period.'"*

An experience like this does not necessarily mean that dating is out of the question. There are a few key approaches you might want to consider.

The most obvious is to ask your friends and family to introduce you to someone who might be compatible with you. Or, you could try the "conventional" approach, which may not be the best approach. Perhaps you may have heard from your friends, parents, or even on TV that you should just walk up to a potential date, say something nice, and if she/he responds positively, you can take it from there. Well, this approach may work, but you have to know what to say, and many of us feel awkward or shy when it comes to making conversation.

You might want to talk to a trusted neurotypical friend or sibling ahead of time, preferably of the same gender and sexual orientation as your potential date, and ask their advice on which conversation starters do and don't work well. You especially will want to think ahead of time about how much about yourself (including the fact that you have NLD) you want to disclose. If the person you are trying to meet does not know that you have NLD or does not understand it, this is a risky option, as he or she may leave or get angry for what seems no reason at all, but that may be "obvious" to him or her, even if it's something as simple as you not making eye contact.

The third approach is to try to nurture an existing close friendship to see if it could become a romantic partnership. The advantage here is that the potential love interest already knows you well enough to understand your NLD, and therefore knows not to read too much into your occasional awkwardness or social gaffes. You will already have established mutual understanding and respect, as well as ways to spend time together—or you wouldn't be friends. The downside is that if the friendship blooms into romance and the romance eventually tanks, you've lost a friend as well as a partner.

And if none of those approaches work, if you are older than 18, you can use an online dating service. Online dating comes in all shapes and sizes. There are the standard "open to everyone" sites (you know, the ones you hear the commercials for), as well as those geared to special interests, race, or religion. There are several sites for those with disabilities, which means both physical and mental disabilities. There is even a website that reviews these disability dating sites.[89] It does not, however, include any sites specifically geared to those with NLD, nor even learning disabilities in general.

So yes, dating is indeed possible for NLDers. In the meantime, though, it is important to know that you don't have to have a boyfriend or girlfriend to be happy. Many of us have found that by engaging in activities we like, we are likely to meet someone with similar interests who also may be interested in us.

When you are ready to begin dating, where can you get additional, reliable information about relationships? And what about the changes of puberty, sex, and sexuality?

The most straightforward and easiest to understand of all the books on the market are The "What's Happening to My Body" Book for Boys[90] and The "What's Happening to My Body" Book for Girls[91] by Lynda Madaras and Area Madaras. Though aimed at younger readers (and you already may be past some of the physical changes the authors describe), these are useful, and answer some of your potentially embarrassing questions in a non-embarrassing way.

For older teens and young adults, good books are Changing Bodies, Changing Lives,[92] by Ruth Bell Alexander, and Our Bodies, Ourselves[93] (which I also recommend for older girls and women). Changing Bodies, Changing Lives covers literally everything you might need to know about sexual development, sexual identity, and sexuality, from how to kiss to the complications of pregnancy. It also addresses other concerns a teen might have, such as eating disorders, how to handle peer pressure, gangs, and drugs and alcohol.

You may have many more questions than have been addressed in this chapter—maybe so many that it would take another whole book to answer them. Fortunately, I can tell you the name of that book: Growing Up on the Spectrum: A Guide to Life, Love, and Learning for Teens and Young Adults with Autism and Asperger's by Lynn Koegel and Claire LaZebnik.[94] This excellent book covers all sorts of things that you need to know, like conversation skills, self-management, bullying, dating, how to throw a party, and much more.

Even if it seems like a lot of trouble now, learning how to make and keep friends is a skill that will benefit you now, and in your adult life. What will your life be like after you graduate from high school? The next chapter will tell you.

Chapter Fourteen

Life After High School

High school graduation day will be here before you know it. Many of your peers may be going off to summer jobs and then college. You know you're smart enough to go to college, if that is your choice, but both your parents—and even you yourself, if you're honest about it—may feel that you are not quite ready to leave home.

It may be painful to hear, but remember that in terms of development, socially and emotionally you may be more like a neurotypical 14-year-old, even though your physical body is now 17 or 18. To give yourself time to catch up, you may need a little more time at home.

Some of the older respondents in this study went directly to college after high school, and fell flat on their faces—not because they couldn't keep up with the academic work, but because their self-discipline and organizational skills just weren't up to speed with their intellectual ability. Living in a dorm while attending college requires all of the above, plus the social savvy to deal with difficult roommates or people in the dorm who are driving you crazy.

I was doing OK in my classes, but the guy who lived in the next room played music all night so I couldn't get any sleep. Every night it was the same thing. Until midnight, he practiced his electric guitar. I tried banging on the walls, reporting him to the RA [Resident Advisor who can resolve conflicts between roommates], but nothing worked. I was exhausted.

I hung out with a bunch of guys who I thought were pretty cool. Two of them seemed normal, but one of them was a stoner, even though it took a while for me to figure it out (I could tell from his glazed eyes and slurred speech). That was OK—I would just leave his room when he lit up. But one night, his mom came to visit. She brought in a pizza, and then opened a beer. I was pretty shocked when she lit up a joint, but then it got worse—she actually came on to me. I started to panic—I didn't know what to do. I tried to find a graceful way to leave, but I couldn't. So I just said, "excuse me" and ran to my room. The worst part was the next day, when I found out that I could have been arrested simply for being in the presence of someone doing drugs, even though I didn't do them.

It's tough to decide whether you are ready to live away from home. One excellent resource is *Leaving Home: Survival of the Hippest* by Andie Parton and Lynn Johnston[95] (the latter is the artist of the comic strip "For Better or For Worse"). The book guides you through the ins and outs of living in a college dorm and in an apartment. It provides lots of great tips on subjects such as weeding out difficult roommates, dealing with landlords, making budgets, and more. Reading it will give you a good overview of the skills you need to live independently, and can help you decide if you feel ready.

For those NLDers who plan to attend college, some of us opted to attend a local two-year or four-year college within commuting distance of home. After the first couple of years, when we had enough experience to understand the demands of college work, we transferred to a different college, or moved onto the campus.

How do you know you are ready for independent living? Below is a checklist. You and your parents may want to tailor it to your specific needs, adding any special issues you may have.

If you can answer "yes" to all these questions, *and* you feel confident about living on your own, you may indeed be ready to live independently.

But if after reading this checklist, you honestly feel that you are not ready to leave home yet, and you are determined to go to college, you might very well consider at least starting your college degree by enrolling in one of the many online programs available.

SELF-ASSESSMENT: ARE YOU READY FOR INDEPENDENT LIVING IN THE DORM?

Academic

- Are all current assignments completely up to date?

- Are you earning a B or better in all your classes? Do you feel you can keep up your grades on your own, without parents reminding you to do your homework or turn in papers?

- Are you keeping a calendar, with all long- and short-term assignments marked, so that you know the deadlines for papers, exams, and projects?

- On your calendar, are you designating appropriate amounts of time during the week in order to complete all assignments thoroughly and on time?

- Have you identified and engaged an appropriate source(s) of extra help (tutor, conference with teachers)?

- Have you availed yourself of the special accommodations offered in class (tutors, extra time for quizzes)?

Personal

- Are you taking excellent care of your health, including taking any meds on time, without reminders from your parents?

- Are you bathing or showering every day?

- Are you brushing and flossing your teeth every day?

- Are you wearing clean underwear, socks, and clothes each day?

- Are you avoiding food and substances harmful to your health?

- Are you consistently making appropriate food choices, in order to maintain a normal weight?

- Have you found an *effective* method for getting eight hours of sleep every night?

- Do you wake up each morning on time, and get right to your daily routine (clean, dress, breakfast, work or class)?

- Do you have a regular exercise plan and implement it daily?

- Are your friends helpful, supportive and generally positive and healthy people?

- Do you have a regular method of stress reduction, such as meditation, prayer, or yoga?

- Do you have a method or support system or person to assist you with any emotional problems/crises?

Applying for college

I know I want to apply to college. But the application process is overwhelming, and I am not sure what I'll find when I get there!

You have to be *really* organized to apply to college, and applying to more than one college is even more challenging. It helps to keep a chart or spreadsheet of all the colleges, their application deadlines (so you can give yourself plenty of time to meet them), the fees, and what else they require, such as essays and letters of reference.

We suggest starting this process no later than the summer before your senior year, so you don't have to be doing applications or writing application essays during the busy fall semester.

Many colleges in the U.S. require the SATs. To prepare for this college entrance exam, you might want to read *Up Your Score: SAT: The Underground Guide*.[96] Written and revised each year by four to six people who aced the SAT, this book gives a funny yet serious guide to the SAT, offers great mnemonics for the vocab words, tips on how and whether to cram, and tells a story about how this torture was thought up by the "Evil Testing Serpent" (ETS).

Also, that very same ETS (which really stands for "Educational Testing Service") has an excellent explanation on its website[97] about what you need to know to document your disability in order to qualify for test accommodations. (Please note that you need to allow several months to get this documentation, send it in, and take the test, so you will want to find out about this process sometime in your sophomore year.)

As you look at potential colleges, how can you tell which ones have the best disability services departments? All colleges and universities are required by law to provide services, but not all do so equally well.

If you are applying to a college in the U.S., an excellent resource is *Learning How to Learn: Getting Into and Surviving College When You Have a Learning Disability* by Joyanne Cobb.[98] While some of the information is now out of date, the back of the book lists all the colleges, ranked by effectiveness and price, that offered good learning disability services at the time the book was written. As you begin an online search for colleges with great disability services, this book will give you an idea of the right questions to ask.

And the beginning of the book gives lots of information on the rights and accommodations to which you are entitled under the ADA and IDEA. The author also reminds you (or more to the point, reminds your parents) that where you get your degree (and what goes on your résumé) does not necessarily have to be the place where you *start* college. So don't stress about getting into the "best" name-brand or Ivy League school right now. You can always transfer later if you qualify and if that's what you want to do.

As far as what to expect at college, another good resource is *College Success for Students with Learning Disabilities.*[99] In addition to giving good advice and lots of helpful hints, the book is really easy to read and to use.

Academics at college

If it hadn't been for the wide variety of online classes at the first college I attended, I don't think I would have finished even the first year.

One thing to keep in mind when choosing a college is that you might do well to find one that offers plenty of online classes. Online classes offer several advantages to those with NLD, as well as those who have restrictive circumstances other than or in addition to NLD, such as part-time work, a child or children, travel, a physical disability, or no means of transportation.

First, since you will be sitting at a computer and not in the classroom, your nonverbal language-reading disability will not get in the way of learning.

Second, because online classes use a discussion forum format, you can reply as often as you want, making your posts as brief or as verbose as you choose, and no one will judge you for being a chatterbox—though if they do, they usually see it as "active participation." When you see the length of other students' posts, you can get a pretty good idea of how much is "too much."

Third, you can replay the audio or video clips as often as you want, whereas in a regular classroom you might be judged negatively for having to have something explained to you again. And there is no need to take notes at all!

Fourth, if you have light-sensitivity issues, and cannot use the computer for long periods of time, you can print out all the posts, look them over one at a time, and write out replies by hand, and then type or dictate them to an aide or a friend later on.

Last, and perhaps most important, online classes have a flexible schedule. Obviously, there are deadlines for assignments and papers, but most are end-of-week, not end-of-day. So you can do the work when it suits you.

NLD in the college classroom

Those who decide to live on campus face the question of whether or not to "self-disclose" their NLD. Whether you choose to tell your professors is up to you. Some people think that their professors might be prejudiced against them if they know they have a disability. But most NLDers feel that it's better to be straightforward because that way, you can get the help you need, plus any accommodations for note-taking or testing, tutors, or any other help that you might need.

> If you are constantly raising your hand in class, but the professor doesn't know you have NLD, he or she might think you are really interested in the class. On the other hand, the professor might just think that you are just a loudmouth. So it's better to tell.

Since it's not that easy to talk about, it might be better to write a letter to your professor telling him or her what you need. To help you get started, here is a sample letter, followed by a couple of samples of the kinds of accommodations you might need.

Dear Mr./Ms./Dr./Professor _____,

I am a freshman this year and I will be taking your class, (*name of class*).

I have Nonverbal Learning Disabilities (NLD), and would greatly appreciate you reading the following information about me, so that we can have a successful semester working together.

I also respectfully request the accommodations listed below. I appreciate your consideration, and welcome any questions you may have. My email is:_____. My cell number is:_____.

Thank you very much,
(Your name)

ABOUT MY LEARNING STYLE AND DISABILITIES

I am a very literal learner. Although I am able to understand abstractions in ideas, I am not that good at inferences. It is helpful to me if assignments and instructions for papers are given in writing and are specific and concrete. The fact that you are using Blackboard [an online learning portal] is a big help to me.

Normally, I do not take many notes in class. This is not because I am not paying attention; I am. When I concentrate, I retain much of what I hear. If the material is also in the textbook or the readings, so much the better. I write very slowly (and not too legibly), so quick note-taking is too hard.

Although I am a lot better than I used to be at reading social cues, I sometimes still miss them. The main implication for your class is that I may not understand when to stop talking, especially if I am passionate about the topic at hand. It would be better for me if you are willing to say something like, "*Name*, we are going to hear from someone else now," or telling someone else, "Let's hear what *you* have to say." If you use nonverbal cues (such as turning your body away from me or looking at another student) I may not be able to understand them. Please don't worry about hurting my feelings by telling me to shut up if necessary (some teachers have worried about this). I would rather you were blunt. This will prevent me from embarrassment and possible censure from fellow students.

Because I have difficulty with executive functioning skills and sequencing, longer written assignments such as those requiring research or multiple steps take me a very long time. I have found that I need to allow one full day to produce a page. Generally this is not a problem, as most professors give such assignments well in advance. In order to produce essays in class, I need a lot of extra time both to organize my thoughts and because I write slowly. I request permission to take midterm and final exams at the Academic Advising Center.

Sample one

Accommodations I will need

1. Midterm and final exam at the Academic Advising Center, as noted above.

2. Extra time to produce any written work (such as quizzes) given in class.

3. To take home assignments, or tests given with sufficient lead time (at least one full day per page required).

Sample two

Accommodations for learning:

1. **Untimed tests** in a distraction-free environment.

2. Limited computer time—to rest my eyes **frequently** (this accommodation is necessary only if there is in-class computer use or tests are given on the computer).

3. **A time management** tutor or "buddy"—for courses with written assignments that extend over time (e.g. papers) and for courses with multiple, simultaneous, written assignments. I need help to look at all assignments, break them down into manageable parts, assign **interim due dates** to each, and report to the tutor or "buddy" as each part is complete. I can do each part without help; it's the overall sequencing and time management that is difficult. For papers, I need some help with **final editing** for continuity and flow. Help is not usually needed for short writing assignments such as those assigned at one class and due at the next, nor for math or science assignments.

4. **Audiobooks** for novels, short stories, longer readings in social sciences. These are not needed for physical sciences or mathematics.

5. I tend to be **very literal**, and take people and things at face value. Sometimes, but not always, this can cause a difficulty in communicating.

Other aspects of college

This may sound silly, but one of the things that really worried me about going to college is the food. I didn't know if there was anything to eat at college besides pizza, fries, and the salad bar.

If you have sensory sensitivity, dining can be a big issue. However, most colleges have a wide selection of food and beverages at every meal, including options for special diets, such as vegetarian, vegan, kosher, and gluten-free. Plus, there are lots of ways to prepare tasty meals from what's available if you don't see something you like.

One of my favorite books is *Tray Gourmet: Be Your Own Chef in the College Cafeteria* by Larry Berger and Lynn Harris.[100] They and various contributing college students provide some rather spectacular and delicious recipes made from the standard cafeteria fare. Recipes range from the simple (making the hard-boiled eggs into deviled eggs, spicing up otherwise boring tuna fish sandwiches, etc.) to making really elaborate burgers, and fancy sundaes for dessert. Even if you don't make the recipes, you still will love many of the names (e.g. "Nietzsche's Nachos" or "Plato's Pita Pocket") and their complementary illustrations by Chris Kalb. The book also gives tips on stuff like dieting (and lack thereof), the pros and cons of caffeine, and how to grow your own culinary herbs.

One good way to eat well and to find out more about what life on campus is like would be to make an in-person visit to the college or colleges you are considering. All colleges have tours and visiting days, and you—and your parents, if they go with you—can ask all the questions you want, both in the admissions office, and from other students you see on your visit.

Alternatives to college

If college isn't right for you, or isn't right for you right now, you have many other post-high-school options. One is a "gap year." Originally started in the UK during the 1970s as a way to fill the "gap" of seven or eight months between final exams and university entrance, a gap year was intended to provide enrichment for the student, usually through international travel. The gap-year concept came to the U.S. in the 1980s, and, today, often includes not only travel, but also structured programs of every kind, including study, volunteer work, internships, and more.

Your gap year could be one semester, a full academic year, or even longer. You may apply to college, get accepted, and then defer for a year. Or you might find that you enjoy what you do directly after high school so much that college loses its immediate appeal. Some NLDers have spent a gap year working in their family business, volunteering in their own community, immersing themselves in learning a foreign language, living on a kibbutz, learning a trade, or starting their own business.

For those who do go on to college, studies show that taking a gap year contributes to a higher grade point average, more maturity, and more readiness for college life.

Job readiness

Some of us with NLD, by choice or by necessity, will be going directly to work right after high school. As much as we'd like to think that we can find a job we truly love, the job we take often is informed by how much money we need to support ourselves, and whether it offers health insurance. So finding a job might be more a matter of practicality than preference.

Here in the U.S., under the provisions of President Obama's Affordable Care Act of 2009, you can be covered on your parents' policy until you are age 26. So that might give you some time to find a job that suits you well, and that you can do with pride.

What kinds of jobs are NLD friendly, and which are not? For the best answer to this question, I refer you to Yvona Fast's *Employment for Individuals With Nonverbal Learning Disabilities and Asperger's Syndrome*.[101] Written by an adult with NLD, this book is by far one of the best NLD-related books on the market. Not only does Fast list good and bad jobs for those with NLD and AS, with clear explanations of what makes them well suited or poorly suited, she also provides the reader with many first-hand testimonies from the NLDers and Aspies about why their current/previous jobs did or did not suit them.

The survey for this edition asked, "If you currently are employed, what is your primary occupation?" Answers were widely varied, and included both blue collar and professional occupations.

Full-time waitress.

Associate editor of a magazine.

Assembly worker.

SAHM (stay-at-home-Mom).

Inventory management.

Attorney.

It also asked, "What, if any, jobs that you have held in the past are particularly NLD-friendly? Which are NLD-unfriendly?"

Floor clerk at Shoppers Drug Mart was NLD-friendly. Laborer at a campsite park position was somewhat NLD-unfriendly. Student job at a community Boys and Girls club was somewhat unfriendly too.

Something without time restraints on completing tasks.

I probably should not be a waitress. It's a miracle I haven't knocked a glass on to anyone.

I've done very well when I was doing various office assistant jobs, both for a nonprofit organization, and also a work-study job that I had in college. Probably the worst job I had was interning in a nursing home.

The job I have now is through a company that employs those on the spectrum. I am one of the few that gets hourly pay. The piece rate I tried I found could never support someone like me who can live independently.

Data entry was pretty good. Customer service (supermarket cashier) was horrible because I couldn't keep my mouth shut when obnoxious, spoiled customers were rude. I got fired for talking back (really, just defending myself, but HR didn't see it that way).

I worked for the tennis coach who had coached me. It was good that he knew me and liked me, but it was not good because I felt badly that I didn't push myself harder.

Sales—NLD-unfriendly. Business analysis and improvement (requires wonderful mentors)—NLD-friendly.

Survey respondents also were asked, "Do you feel that your NLD makes it challenging to find work? Why or why not?" They said:

Yes. I haven't been working while in school because my executive functioning issues have made it hard to juggle working and school.

Finding the job is not the problem—it's keeping it.

Yes—I am going to have a harder time interviewing, I think, and I don't have good enough skills yet in learning how to work with co-workers.

I know this sounds strange, but I think the NLD makes it easier to work; it's just the epilepsy that I also have that makes it damn near impossible.

Yes, feeling motivated can be sometimes difficult.

Probably, unless the directions given are very, very clear. I had a lot of difficulty holding down a job because if what the boss said didn't make sense to me it was hard—sometimes impossible—for me to do it and then I would get reprimanded.

Yes. I don't interview well.

Tough question because NLDers can possess presentation skills which can make their "faking it" during interviews seem they are perfectly qualified for jobs. I've done this and suffered greatly after being "found out." The best advice is to have people with experience help you prepare for different environments and situations.

NLD made it very hard to complete my master's degree in education. Instead of graduating with my professional license, I was unable to advance to the practicum needed for the license.

Yes, social skills were a challenge.

Yes, social and sensory issues made it tough to work.

I did very well in college—all the way through completing my master's degree, because I knew exactly what was expected, and most everything was very orderly. I am finding it more difficult to succeed in the workplace because "office politics" is something I just have a tough time figuring out.

Legal protection on the job

If you live in the U.S., are fortunate enough to find a job that suits you, but encounter workplace discrimination because of your NLD, are you protected under the ADA?

This is an interesting question, and one that requires a bit of explanation and some background history, especially considering that the status of NLD as a "real" learning disability is still in question. (See Chapter Sixteen for more information on this.)

The roots of the ADA lie in the Rehabilitation Act of 1973, a civil rights statute for government workers and contractors, and people who received government-granted financial aid, all of whom had disabilities (then called "handicaps").[102] It is from the Rehabilitation Act that the term and idea of "being on disability" came about, meaning that one was receiving aid from the government, either permanently or until such time as the individual was able to work again.

Then, in 1989, came the proposal of the ADA. Its premise was to protect people with disabilities from discrimination. It received strong bipartisan support in both the House and the Senate, and when President Bush signed it into law on July 26, 1990, he and the vast majority of Congress were pleased. Senator Orrin Hatch (R-Utah) called it "historic legislation." The late Senator Edward Kennedy (D-Massachusetts) even went so far as to call it an "emancipation proclamation" for people with disabilities.[103]

Yet a 2000 survey showed that 97 percent of disability-based employment discrimination lawsuits were ruled in favor of the employer.[104] So what went wrong?

When the ADA was drafted, it defined the term "disability" in the exact words the Rehabilitation Act used to define the term "handicap:"

> (1) a physical or mental impairment that substantially limits one or more of the major life activities of such an individual; (2) a record of such an impairment; or (3) being regarded as having such impairment.[105]

Not too much to worry about, right? But remember back to Chapter One, regarding what the "D" in "LD" stands for, that: "…labeling it a 'disability' makes it sound as though you once had the ability, but were rendered inoperative?" Well, that was the problem.

The courts determined that the phrase "substantially limits one or more of the major life activities" should be taken as literally and seriously as possible (since government payments were at stake), thereby making it nearly impossible for many people to prove that they had a disability. But what got completely lost in the process was the fact that these were not meant to be subsidy cases eligible for government benefits; they were meant to be civil rights cases. The plaintiffs did not want to be out of work collecting government money; they wanted to be back at the jobs they had before they were fired unjustly. Clearly, this had to be corrected somehow.

Enter the 2008 Americans with Disabilities Act Amendments Act (ADAAA), which was passed a mere six weeks after the first edition of this book was published, and became effective on January 1, 2009.

The first major change from the old ADA is that the ADAAA now covers those with disabilities that were once not "major enough" to "substantially limit" an individual's life or lifestyle. The new conditions covered include, but are not limited to: HIV, epilepsy, intellectual and developmental disabilities, post-traumatic stress disorder, diabetes, multiple sclerosis,[106] heart attacks, bipolar disorder, major depressive disorder, needing an oxygen tank, vertigo, back injury, and anxiety.[107]

So, what does all this mean for someone with NLD? As to the original question of whether you are protected under the ADA, the answer is: you didn't used to be, but now you probably are.

Probably.

If you encounter workplace discrimination and/or are fired because you have NLD:

1. find a good learning disability advocacy lawyer

2. have handy a copy of your most recent diagnostic write-up

3. have some other official resource that proves that NLD qualifies as an "intellectual or developmental disability."

If all that does not work, you could try your claim on the basis of some other condition you may have, like anxiety. For more information, contact the Equal Employment Opportunity Council.[108] To find out more about the history of the ADA, go to its website.[109]

If you are unable to work

Those of us with NLD who may be unable to work, or who may not be able to work full time, are at a disadvantage when it comes to saving for our future. If we don't work, we don't contribute into the Social Security system, as do our working peers. We also cannot put money into Roth IRAs or other tax-advantaged savings accounts, which depend on earned income. We may get years behind in our retirement savings—not something most of us worry about when we are in high school. But it is important, because compound interest on our savings throughout the years is a key factor in having enough money to live on when we are old.

In terms of financial planning, your family might want to look into setting up a "Supplemental Needs Trust," which protects assets for your use in case you are now receiving or may ever need to receive government disability assistance. You will need to discuss this issue with an attorney, preferably one who specializes in the area of "Elder Law."[110]

In terms of health insurance, again, you can remain on your parents' policy until you are 26. However, most insurance companies also have a clause that will cover a "disabled dependent child" of any age. As long as you are single, not working, and living at home, you may be eligible to remain on your parents' policy past that age. However, not all of us are comfortable with that nomenclature. We don't like to think of ourselves as "disabled" or "dependent," but if we are unable to work, and with the price of insurance going up rapidly, it is something to consider.

Military service

Although I personally do not know of any NLDer in the service, to the best of my knowledge, there is no law that prevents you from joining if you want to serve. However, certain academic skills deficits, as well as the current use of medication to improve academic skills, likely will disqualify you for military service. Also, unlike at college, the military does not have to make accommodations, either for the entrance tests or during service.

On the other hand, the structure, rules, and very clear expectations of the military may suit an individual with NLD very well. You yourself and perhaps the recruiting staff will have to determine whether any problems you may have, such as difficulty with visual–spatial skills or adapting to new situations—such as suddenly finding yourself being shipped out to another country—might make service difficult.

Whatever life after high school might bring you—whether college, online learning, a gap year, employment, or the military—understand that, in terms of the development of NLD symptoms, it's all likely to get better from here, even if it doesn't seem that way immediately. Chapter Fifteen shows why.

Chapter Fifteen

It's a Wonderful Life—
Even with NLD

Now that you have read our best tips and strategies for dealing with some of the more challenging aspects of NLD, you may want to think more about your future. What is adult life like when you have a disability?

> *I know that it's hard for you, but it's not always going to be this bad. Some of the symptoms ease up over the years, and you learn to adapt and compensate for your weaknesses, and build on your strengths. Plus, high school sucks for everyone, and life gets better once you get out of high school.*

> *Even if I had known [about having NLD] earlier, I think the maturity of adolescence was required for the type of serious introspection and self-analysis that I have done in the past two to three years.*

Creating a happy life for yourself

From talking with dozens of other young adults with NLD, here is more about what I've learned and you might want to know about creating a full, rich life for yourself. (If you are a neurotypical parent reading this, these simple "rules" may be obvious to you. But those of us with NLD don't necessarily grasp them intuitively.)

1: You need just one living being who loves you and whom you love in return

This can be a parent, sibling, or grandparent, an aunt, uncle, or cousin, or other family member. It can be a best friend or spouse, or anyone else with whom you have a strong and loyal connection. Notice I didn't say "boyfriend," or "girlfriend." If you have a significant other in your life right now, that's great, but that relationship is likely to change as you change and grow. So it's best not to depend on a love interest as your "one person" unless you are married to them. (And, as many of the survey respondents, whose parents are divorced, know all too well, even marriage isn't necessarily a lifelong relationship anymore.)

> *I don't have a lot of friends, but I have one best friend, who has been my best friend since kindergarten. She doesn't have NLD, but she totally "gets" who I am. Plus, my parents, even though we don't always get along, are always here for me.*

2: Find at least one positive and healthy thing you really love to do

This can be something physical, like a sport; or mental, like doing the *New York Times* Sunday crossword puzzle, or Sudoku, or chess. Or it could be something artistic, like painting, or building miniatures for dollhouses. Or musical, like playing in a band, or even just listening to the oldies station for so long that you become an expert on rock music.

> *Be yourself. Find something you love and do it with all your energy.*

> *Work and love are both important. But if you had to pick just one, I'd go for work or a hobby every time. Work doesn't forget to call. Work rarely disappoints you. Work doesn't tease you or call you names. If you have a problem with work, the answer depends on you. What you put into your work is pretty much what you will get out. Unlike love, which can be unpredictable.*

The survey asked, "What do you love to spend time doing?" The answers were as varied as the respondents:

> *Reading.*

> *Learning about foreign cultures.*

> *Playing Scrabble, playing games, doing crosswords, Sudoku, puzzle magazine puzzles.*

> *Swimming, walking, movies, reading.*

Making all kinds of lists of pop music ("best ofs," "worst ofs," bands that should tour together based on their names).

Gardening. Playing with my daughter. Volunteering at the school.

Time with my family, and learning new things.

I like to do counted cross stitch and other crafty things.

Relaxing. Clearing my head.

Reading, exercising.

Reading, writing, and listening to music.

Finding one thing you love to do often leads right into the next element of a happy life…

3: Find a community where you feel valued and where you belong

This can be related to the one thing you really love to do, or to another passion. Being a valued member of a group you respect and with which you can connect makes you feel good about yourself and about your future.

I attend religious services weekly. When I walk into the Sanctuary, I am greeted by at least 45 people who know me and who make me feel like I am not only welcome there, but that my presence really matters.

When I joined the literary magazine at college, I found myself among a group of like-minded people with a common goal: to publish an irreverent, entertaining journal. I really looked forward to the meetings. I felt welcome and important, especially when my stories got in print.

4: Find a way to be productive

You may not realize it now, but sometimes, you can turn your skills and talents into useful work—either paid or volunteer. The survey asked, "What do you feel are your greatest talents?" NLDers said:

The study of linguistics.

Leading a Bible Study group at my house of worship.

Listening. Being able to laugh at myself. Resilience.

Art, writing, reading, learning.

I am kind. I try to be sensitive and a good listener.

That I am humble enough not to answer this question.

I'm a talented singer and actor. I'm also very caring and compassionate.

Anything lexicological.

Cooking. I especially like making dinner for my family.

Persistence.

Writing.

Whether you are studying for a diploma or a degree, working as a bagger in the local supermarket, or volunteering to cook or serve dinner at a homeless shelter, you are giving of yourself and making the world a little bit better. However small your efforts may seem, they really matter. No one on this planet has the exact combination of gifts and talents and strengths that you have. You *can* make a difference in the world—so go do it.

I work at Pet Pals shelter on Saturdays, helping to feed and water the animals, and even cleaning up the cages and stuff. This is the best part of my week, and I'm always sad and happy at the same time when one of my favorite dogs or kittens gets adopted. I wish I could take them all home with me.

Because of having NLD, I really didn't think that there was any organization that would want me as a volunteer, because my people skills aren't that great. But I was really surprised to find out from my math teacher that if you are good on a computer, there are a lot of organizations that can use your help. She helped me to connect with a local battered women's shelter. I now work in the office two days a week after school, helping them with mailings to donors and entering the gifts into their database. The next project is they are going to let me work on redesigning their website! I am so happy that I can contribute to a cause I believe in.

5: Have a dream and work toward it

What do you want to do with your life? Although you may not recognize this right now, those unique talents and gifts can be shared in service to others or parlayed into a career, or both. Perhaps you are one of the lucky ones: you already know that you are a talented artist, or a whiz with computers, or that you have a gentle touch with animals, or you make the best cupcakes in town:

> When I was in high school, my parents were so focused on me getting into a "good" college that I didn't think I had the option not to go to college at all. But the one thing that brings me the most joy is baking—everything from simple breads and muffins to fancy party desserts. After spending two miserable years in a college that was all wrong for me, I dropped out and got a job at the local bakery. After a while, the owner urged me to apply to a culinary arts program, so I did, majoring in Baking and Pastry Arts. I'll graduate soon, and already have half a dozen job offers doing what I love best!

> My work at the pet shelter has been so satisfying that I am seriously considering going to college, and then on to veterinary school. It would be my dream job to help heal sick or injured animals.

It is important to take pride in and to celebrate your accomplishments along the way. All the subjects had at least one goal he or she had reached that greatly improved their self-esteem, and view of the world, and actually made them feel happier.

> One of my favorite [accomplishments] is that in college so far I've made the Dean's List twice… And to make the Dean's List at this university, you need to have a 3.5 or higher and no incompletes, and full-time status, a minimum of 12 credits. I've also made improvements in social areas too.

> After basically flunking out of two colleges, after I got my diagnosis, I entered [a local] community college and graduated with my Associates degree summa cum laude.

> I trained for six months for a 10k race for women. Of course I didn't win, not even close, but I finished in a respectable (for me) time. For someone who grew up knowing she was a total klutz, this really changed the way I see myself. I now feel I can do almost anything!

And many of us have goals we are working towards, or hope to achieve someday. The survey asked, "What difference do you want to make in the world?" Our goals ranged from *advocacy*:

Advocate for policy change for disabled persons.

I really want to make all strobe lights on government vehicles illegal so that people with epilepsy can drive.

I want to help others to see autistics through my eyes if it'll help stop bullying.

To *career-specific:*

I want to open up the Jewish canon to reintroduce erstwhile banned texts.

To build an underground amusement park.

To earn my law degree.

I want to make a fun center type place for those on the spectrum.

To own my own business, though I don't yet know what that will be.

To *philosophical:*

I don't believe I am in a position to make a difference in the world by myself. I believe we must all join in unity to change the world.

Help people.

To a focus on the *next generation:*

To raise my child to believe in herself.

The lives of my children.

I'm a teacher. I hope to mold the minds of young people and teach them how to be responsible, curious people.

Perhaps you have many different interests and skills, but have not yet discovered the one thing that makes you want to get up and get going in the morning. So how can you find it? One tool we have found useful is to spend some time thinking about your life and what you want from it. What does having NLD mean to you? What will it mean as you grow up?

Reflections on growing up with NLD

Most of those who contributed to this book have spent some time reflecting on what it means to have NLD. These reflections took many different forms. Most respondents have discussed their condition with parents (65%), siblings or other relatives (30%), with friends who have NLD (35%) and those who do not (39%), teachers (26%), and therapists, counselors or religious leaders (57%).

These conversations are not always easy or simple:

> [I've done] a whole lot of introspection. I have on occasion discussed [having NLD] to a limited extent with parents and friends but it is still extremely uncomfortable for me to do so.

We also spent time in self-reflection, expressing ourselves through journal writing (48%), meditation (17%), song or poetry writing (22%), painting, drawing or sculpture (9%), or through the performing arts (26%). Others reported the following:

> Internal self-reflection (reflecting on the nature of my condition without writing anything down).

> Learning more about it and educating others.

> Discuss with husband.

> Learning about NLD and disabilities in general.

Another method of self-reflection—and a good way for us to help others—is to think about and share what we've learned about growing up with NLD. The survey asked, "What would you tell a young friend or relative who just found out they have NLD?" Our answers ranged from the *very specific*:

> I'd just give them a PDA and show them how to use it. It would come in handy.

> Get in LD classes.

> Try to take the ACT instead of the SAT. [ACT: American College Testing. This is basically a test a high school student might substitute for the SAT, in order to get into college.] When you are applying to grad school, try to find a school that accepts the Miller Analogy Test rather than the GREs—much easier. [GRE: Graduate Record Examination.

*This is the primary test college students take to get into graduate school.]
Just as the ACT acts as substitute for the SAT, college students can opt
for the Miller Analogies Test (MAT) instead of the GRE.*

*I would like to add some advice: start at a community college and let
them know about your disability, and then go for a four-year degree.*

*Go to the State Vocational Rehabilitation people for funding for college
and help with job finding and coaching after you get out of college.*

To the *philosophical*:

*Try to find a happy medium between blending in with the crowd and
going your own way. Social isolation only compounds depression.*

That everything goes up from here!

Just be yourself, and don't worry about the other kids teasing you.

To a *combination* of both:

*I would certainly like to spend more time with them and observe them
and hope to be able to give them advice along the way. I probably
wouldn't tell them anything initially because I don't want my informing
them about their NLD to become a self-fulfilling prophecy. I have been
extremely cautious (as much as humanly possible) to make absolutely sure
that I do not limit myself by talking myself into anything. I have to make
sure with several examples that I have been insurmountably limited by a
certain element of my NLD.*

*It's not the end of the world. Get therapy and intervention. Skip classes
if you want to. Skip gym. Watch fashions and dress to blend in but don't
follow the crowd. You could have it way worse. You can learn to hide
NLD, but you'd never be able to hide a wheelchair. NLD is just one
tiny part of who you are, and it has nothing to do with your soul or
personality. It's just a disability. You'll always be yourself first.*

*That I have it too. I understand what they are going through and I
can help them find ways to compensate through school and finding an
advocate to help them out throughout the years, including job hunting.*

*I would tell them to get interventions immediately with all of the resources
they have. The younger they start, the more they'll see improvement. I'd
encourage them to be an advocate for themselves and never let their rights*

be denied. Finally, I'd tell them not to give up hope—things get better as you get older.

The survey also asked, "What do you wish you'd known earlier?" The answers were both poignant and practical:

I wish I had had the diagnosis of NLD when I was younger so that I could have received interventions and a greater understanding of self from a young age.

I wish I had known I wasn't a bad kid or a stupid kid and that some things were out of my control.

[I wish I'd known earlier] that I would need things said to me in words.

I would have loved to have known earlier in my childhood that I had NLD because then I could have gotten accommodations and learned how I need to learn.

That I'm not stupid. And I'm not weird for looking at things differently.

That I had [NLD], so teachers could adjust tests, and I wouldn't have had to take a Special Ed class.

[I wish I'd known] the possible outcomes that could have resulted. What could have happened had I NOT gone into Special Ed. What could have happened had I received a correct diagnosis sooner.

I wish I had known about my various disorders and how they affect me. My ADHD wasn't treated until I was 14, social phobia wasn't treated until I was 17. I wish I had known about NLD, that I wasn't just a total failure.

I don't know…we knew a lot about my disabilities very early on. (They just didn't have a real name.) Maybe that I wasn't really epileptic and didn't need anti-convulsant meds, though.

That I had [NLD], that a lot of the things that happened were not my fault and that there is nothing wrong with me.

To self-advocate, tell other people that you don't understand them and that you are different from typical people, and you need to learn in a different way.

That the NLD itself is not nearly as disabling as the more all-encompassing "SPED mindset"—that you are stupid, wrong, incompetent, deficient, crazy, etc.

I wish I had the social skills as a kid that I do now as an adult.

I wish I knew the process I have taught myself, how to learn.

Things get easier.

Coping skills.

I wish I'd known absolutely everything that was going to happen in my life, down to the last second, of course! Then I could expect it! But I'm being facetious. I wish I'd known that it takes a lot to kill a person. You are stronger than you realize. No matter what you're going through, somebody else has it worse. Every second will pass, every hour will pass, every day will pass, eventually.

I am content with how my life has shaped up. If I hadn't gone through everything I have and will I would not be the person I am today.

[I wish I'd known earlier] that I am fine the way I am, that some of the challenges of having NLD will resolve with time, and that my life is what I make of it!

There *is* more to you than your NLD, though sometimes it may not feel that way. The symptoms, limitations, and challenges may feel so overwhelming that it is easy to lose sight of the whole, unique person you are—NLD and all. As you grow to adulthood, it is important to be mindful that things do get better over time for most of us.

Part V

The Big Questions

Chapter Sixteen

The Politics of NLD

In the second edition of this book, I answered the most frequently asked questions sent in by readers of the first edition. Most of these pertained to specific, practical matters. Since the publication of that edition, readers have asked many more "big picture" existential questions—which will be addressed here.

Is NLD real? (It's not clear)

Having read this far, your answer most likely is: "Well, *of course* it is!" But pause for a moment and consider this: NLD is a syndrome that's talked about, written about, and recognized by SPED teachers, psychologists, self-identified "LD advocates," therapists, and other professionals. And yet, NLD has never made it into the APA's Diagnostic and Statistical Manual of Mental Disorders (DSM), the handbook that lists different categories of mental disorders and how to diagnose them.

The more recent edition, the DSM-5, published in 2013, does not include it. NLD is not mentioned at all in either the 1990 or 2004 version of the IDEA. It's not mentioned in either the original 1990 or the most recent 2008 version of the ADA. It's not even mentioned by the National Institutes of Health (NIH) or the National Institute of Mental Health (NIMH), both of which tend to be very strong critics of the DSM.

None of these institutions, nor any legislative body, mentions NLD—none at all. So how can it be real? Is NLD the psychological equivalent of the Zen koan: "If a tree falls in the forest and no one hears it, does it make a sound?"

If NLD is not officially recognized, however, then how do you explain that to someone who's been diagnosed with it, or to their parents, or teachers? How would it be explained to those who write books about it? Could an "imaginary" condition generate hundreds of emails from grateful NLDers and parents, who say, "Finally! Someone who gets it!"? Are we all making this up?

But if NLD *is* real, then why isn't it being recognized? To be "officially" recognized, a learning or psychological disorder has to be included in the DSM. To be tracked in the classroom via the IDEA, or in the workplace via the ADA, NLD first would have to be in the DSM.

Many think that NLD may make it into the next edition (DSM-6), or in a revision of the current edition. But until then, NLD is not considered a "real" disorder, and cannot be diagnosed as such, if tests or services are required, because when it comes to mental health issues, most insurance companies will pay only for services relating to "official" DSM disorders.

Therefore, it is common practice among psychologists who administer the diagnostic tests for NLD to give the results a different label, so that their patient or client can get the help and services he or she needs.

Because this is the case, it can become extremely confusing to the (otherwise-labeled) NLDer and his/her family, who might not even know if what is presented by the psychologist is the right diagnosis, or if there even is a specific, identifiable problem.

So why isn't NLD "official"? Read on.

The ADD bloc(k)

ADD, later called "ADHD"—first with parentheses around the "H," then with a diagonal slash, and then without any punctuation—has been in the public eye since the 1980s. As soon as it was included in the DSM, those who were diagnosed with ADD began to benefit (or not, depending on your point of view) from heightened media attention, including books, articles, videos, and conferences on how to recognize it, treat it, medicate it—you name it. Many "women's magazines"—the ones that moms read—suddenly began including ads for ADD meds: first Ritalin, then Adderall and Vyvanse, and others. Certainly, some of these medications can help with some ADD symptoms, and if those who have ADD need them, that's a decision for them and their doctors to make.

But it seems curious that, as soon as there was money to be made for a "cure," ADD made it into the DSM. The APA could have mentioned ADD in the DSM-I, but at the time, the confluence of the APA's focus on psychoanalysis as the primary focus of psychiatry, and the limited exposure of Dr. Charles Bradley's experiments in administering Benzedrine to hyperactive children in 1937[111] did not support furthering ADD awareness.

However, since the FDA's approval of Ritalin in 1955,[112] the success rate, and therefore, the prescriptions of medicine to treat ADD, has risen steadily. So when the DSM-II came out in 1968, ADD was included, albeit under the name "hyperkinetic impulse disorder."

Then, in the 1980 DSM-III, the name was changed to ADD with two subtypes: "with hyperactivity" and "without hyperactivity." In the 1987 DSM-III-R, the name was changed to ADHD, and the diagnosis combined the two subtypes into one, with three symptoms: inattentiveness, impulsivity, and hyperactivity. Then the DSM-IV in 1994, continued with the DSM-IV-TR in 2000, went back to subtypes, this time three instead of two: combined type ADHD, predominantly inattentive type ADD, and predominantly hyperactive-impulse type ADHD, which has, for the most part, remained the model for ADHD in the DSM-5.

The Autism bloc(k)s

And what of Autism Spectrum Disorders? The history of autism is long and complex, and the vast majority of it is well beyond the scope of this book, but I strongly suggest that if you really want to know the full history—everything from the development of the puzzle piece logo to the MMR vaccine controversy to autistic geniuses who invented and/or discovered such scientific breakthroughs as the basis of the periodic table and properties of electricity, to online research staples like Wikipedia and JSTOR—that you read *Neurotribes: The Legacy of Autism and the Future of Neurodiversity* by Steve Silberman.[113]

But in order to get a better understanding of NLD, it is truly important to understand the history of how autism is diagnosed.

The first mention of autism was in 1911 by Swiss eugenicist psychologist Eugen Bleuler, who, in his *Dementia Praecox, oder Gruppe der Schizophrenien* (Dementia Praecox, or the Group of Schizophrenias), used it as one of several aspects of schizophrenia (another term he coined) to mean self-centered reflection and retreat into fantasy.

Not until 1943, when Leo Kanner—a German-born Jewish psychologist, who managed to escape the Nazis in 1937, along with Sigmund Freud and several other Jewish medical notables—published his paper, "Autistic Disturbances of Affective Conduct," was the diagnosis for (infantile/low-functioning) autism put forth. It was characterized primarily by, "inability to relate themselves in the ordinary way to people and situations from the beginning of life," "extreme autistic aloneness," and "an anxiously obsessive desire for the maintenance of sameness." In 1944, when the paper made it into *Pediatrics Magazine*, Kanner officially called it "early infantile autism."[114]

Meanwhile, in Vienna, Hans Asperger crafted his *Autistischen Psychopathen*, published in 1944, which, despite the "psychopathy" in the name, painted a much different picture than did Kanner. Asperger, effectively, said that:

- autism could present itself in many different ways, at many different levels of intelligence

- it is not just limited to childhood

- it runs in the family

- it's almost exclusively found in males

- and, most important of all, there exists an "autistic intelligence"—a combination of creativity, questioning conventional wisdom, and determination.[115]

But Kanner, despite praising one of Asperger's mentors—hence proving that he was at least aware of Asperger's work[116]—tried to write Asperger out of history by accusing him of being a Nazi sympathizer, even though Asperger's clinic was burned down by the Nazis because it housed both the "feebleminded" and Jews—both prime Nazi targets.

By the time the DSM-II came out in 1968, without an entry for autism, but with one for "childhood schizoid disorder" (a nod to Eugen Bleuler), many psychologists were trying to figure out why this strange disorder came about. One of the predominant theories, most notably put forth by Bruno Bettelheim, was that it had to be the fault of cold, aloof, borderline negligent parents. By "parents," he meant "mothers."

Naturally, this upset many mothers of autistic children, and no one more so than a British doctor named Lorna Wing. Along with her husband, John Wing, and her colleague, Judith Gould, she undertook an investigative study in the UK of subjects who showed any of Kanner's signs of autism, and any of Asperger's signs, and at what age the symptoms first appeared.

Much as Asperger had predicted, she found that some qualities of autism remain throughout the affected individual's lifespan, but these qualities or symptoms may lessen dramatically over time. Thus, Dr. Wing created the notion of an "autistic spectrum," while fighting to restore Asperger's good name, by first calling her findings "Asperger's Syndrome."

At the time the DSM-III was rolled out in the U.S. in 1980, the only progress the APA had made was to honor Kanner with an entry for "infantile autistic disorder." It was not until the release of the movie *Rain Man* in 1988—which relied on the expertise of American researchers Dr. Oliver Sacks and Temple Grandin—that America finally woke up to the fact that there is a "high-functioning" version of autism.

It took the APA until 1994 to list an entry for Asperger's Syndrome in the DSM-IV along with "autistic disorder" (and many, many, other autism-ish entries ending in "—Not Otherwise Specified," which became much harder to diagnose with the 2000 DSM-IV-TR). But until then, throughout the 1990s, there was a big to-do about "Is it Asperger's, or is it high-functioning autism?"

From the publication of the DSM-IV until the publication of the DSM-5, it was referred to as "Asperger's Syndrome." As time went on, prevalent thought was, "Well, a lot of these disorders in the DSM-IV have a lot of the same symptoms as Autism, and can be grouped together. And we really need to call them 'Autism Spectrum Disorders' because there's some kind of a spectrum going on here."

This was in spite of the fact that it was not exactly clear what that "spectrum" is, based on seven or eight disabilities that share a handful of similar characteristics, and which defied Lorna Wing's original vision of an autistic continuum, just as the DSM-IV definition of Asperger's Syndrome didn't line up with Hans Asperger's descriptions of his patients.

Nevertheless, various autism advocacy groups kept pushing and, all of a sudden, by the time of the publication of the DSM-5, "autistic disorder" got isolated, only to be replaced with "Autism Spectrum Disorder" ("ASD" singular). Asperger's Syndrome and all the "–NOS" disorders disappeared, subsumed into "ASD," which had multiple tiers of severity. While there definitely are ways of measuring the severity of these tiers, what prompted the names or need for them is unclear.

Should NLD be considered an ASD?

In the opinion of many NLDers, the DSM is way, way, WAY behind the times. While there definitely are elements of political and financial motivation, the problem lies mostly in the DSM's history of cultural lag. For example, the "mental disorder" "homosexuality" was one of the first entries in the DSM-I (in 1952), and remained there until May of 1974, in the seventh revision of the second edition, when laypeople and clinicians were finally successful in demanding its removal.

So, should NLD be considered an Autism Spectrum Disorder? The U.S. Department of Health and Human Services Centers for Disease Control and Prevention (CDC)[117] does not include Nonverbal Learning Disabilities in its definition of Autism Spectrum Disorders. But some experts say it should be included.

I thought it would be valuable to get some input on this question from those with Asperger's Syndrome as well. One friend with Asperger's I asked said:

The main difference that makes Asperger's count as "sort of autistic" is that in AS there is an element of obsessive-compulsive disorder which you won't find in NLD.

Recently retired SPED teacher Gayle Alexander, M.A.Ed., says:

Each year, I grew more baffled by the distinction between NLD and Asperger's. I have not found a definitive answer to this and I have searched for years. For me, the labels are useful in that they give me an idea of what support these individuals may or may not need. Both diagnoses often require very similar interventions and support systems, but it is not until I worked with students that I could determine, through trial and error, what is truly helpful.[118]

I think it is most important to hear directly from those with NLD, because it is my strong feeling that *we* NLDers should get to define ourselves. So the survey asked, "Is NLD an Autism Spectrum Disorder?" Like the professionals' answers, the respondents' answers varied greatly. Many respondents said some variation of, "I am not sure," or "I don't know," or "I don't know what that is," or "I haven't really thought about this."

The rest had strong opinions on both sides of the issue:

Yes, I see NLD on the mild end of the autistic spectrum. I see NLD as having many similar features to other autistic spectrum disorders, and I have related to individuals I've known with Asperger's Syndrome. I also think NLD would get more publicity and recognition [if it were] on the spectrum.

Yes. I have MUCH more in common with your average autistic person than I do with your average neurotypical. Also many people with NLD, myself included, have serious sensory issues which are on the spectrum. Calling it an LD makes people think it only exists in school. When I say it is an ASD, people understand more and understand how hard stuff can be for me.

No. I don't. Because if it were only the case that the aspect of social cue misreading was in question, then you could base an entire spectrum of disorders around that, but calling it an ASD is insinuating that to be NLD, you are "somewhat autistic," and that's not only a misnomer, it's grossly misleading.

No. NLD has some similar characteristics but it is different.

The ONLY things NLD and autism have in common are the aspects of having poor executive functioning skills, and being "behind the curve" in terms of social skills. But even then, a lot of us with NLD do have friends, and a lot of the time, all "poor social skills" amounts to for NLDers is being an introvert.

I think, if enough NLD symptoms overlap with autism symptoms, the result is Asperger's, which is why Asperger's is so often confused with both. Maybe there should be an Asperger's syndrome spectrum, with NLD at one end and autism at the other. Maybe that might be a little more plausible.

I'm not sure, I'm not a neurologist. If I were to claim that it should be considered part of the autistic spectrum because of afflicted trait x, it's pure opinion. The autistic spectrum should be defined on a purely neurological level.

I used to think that it should and I often fantasized about being able to tell people that I have autism and the instant recognition and resonation that would come along with it. However, I am a part of an online NLD community and I have read some very persuasive arguments as to the negative impact of NLD being grouped along with autism. Overall, I do not have a definitive opinion on the matter because of the overwhelming difficulty of defining the terms "autism" and "nonverbal learning disability."

For me no. Maybe some people with NLD also have a spectrum disorder but not everyone.

Yes and no—it should always be looked for, evaluated in someone with an ASD, but it can be present in people who don't have ASD.

I don't think there should be any such thing as an "autism spectrum." What is it a spectrum of?

I think it is a little different than autism but in a lot of ways the same. It depends on the person.

I don't think so. Never really gave it much thought.

Tough one, as there are so many similarities except for the verbal component.

Yes, there are many parts that overlap. I still struggle when speaking with monitoring the way my words come out and the tone of voice I'm using.

One answer sums it up really nicely:

No. I think there are major problems with a system that offers services based on people's labels instead of what they actually need.

So even though the evidence is not conclusive as to whether NLD and Asperger's Syndrome are the same, whether NLD should be considered an Autism Spectrum Disorder, whether NLD is a subset of Asperger's Syndrome or vice versa, or whether NLD overlaps with, or is a subset of, ADD, at least you now have far more information from which to draw your own conclusion.

Should NLD be in the DSM?

The survey asked, "NLD has never been mentioned in any version of the APA's Diagnostic and Statistical Manual of Mental Disorders (DSM). Do you think it should be? Why or why not?" NLDers said:

Absolutely, I emailed 15 therapists once trying to get help and only one had even heard of it. Maybe helping children early will make a difference in their adult lives.

Yes—if that book is actually helpful to diagnosticians, because it always helps to have a more definitive understanding of specific problems, or shades thereof.

Yes, due to its finite, and clear differences of certain behavioral and cognitive traits.

Well, it's not a mental disorder, it's a learning disability. But I believe the DSM contains other learning disabilities, so why exclude it?

Yes, if only to raise awareness.

Probably not. It's not yet understood.

Yes. It should be more specific.

Proposing a radical revamping of the NLD diagnosis

What if it could be different? What if, as of the next revision or edition of the DSM, there could be an entry for NLD: not called "NLD," but "NLD Spectrum Disorder?"

First, framing it as "NLD Spectrum Disorder" would presuppose that both ADD and Asperger's are dropped as diagnoses, and inserting their respective symptoms into the NLD spectrum. That is, almost any and every one of the symptom areas that have traditionally defined ADD and Asperger's also overlap with NLD, so if one were to simply apply them to NLD, they would still fit the NLD diagnosis. Although ADD and Asperger's intersect at a few points, picturing that intersection on a Venn diagram, NLD—far from merely being the intersection—is instead the greater circle around the circles of ADD and Asperger's. That is, NLD encompasses both.

Aside from the overlap with NLD, there is so much overlap between the symptomology of ADD and Autism Spectrum Disorders, defined both clinically and colloquially. What do people in both of these groups have in common? When they break rules, it is not because they are willfully disobedient, but either because they don't understand the rule, or they don't understand the rationale behind the rule. Both are highly motivated by a need for clarity, justice, logic, and equity. Individuals with ADD and with Asperger's tend to struggle with social cues, can be chatterboxes, and don't know when to stop talking. Both can have problems with motor skills, with executive functioning and prioritization, and all of this—*all of this*—is part of what defines NLD.

In trying to determine where each disorder might depart from the other, people might say things like, "ADD kids do not do that 'stim' thing; they don't have hypersensitivity to sensory input," or "Aspies don't have hyperactivity," but in both cases, NLDers very well might. While NLD might not be defined as "engaging in self-stimulating behaviors," or hypersensitivity, or hyperactivity, a lot of NLDers have these symptoms nonetheless.

The only point at which ADD could break from NLD and be called something else is where it intersects with bipolar disorder, much in the same way that the only point at which Asperger's could break from NLD is when it becomes straight-up autism.

Using a conservative estimate, perhaps if 25 percent each of those with ADD and Asperger's were so severe in their respective diagnoses that they really needed a different diagnosis (such as bipolar disorder or autism) then the remaining 75 percent of each group could instead have been diagnosed with NLD.

What does this mean? Although, as you read in Chapter Two, NLDers are said to comprise between 0.5 percent and 1.5 percent of the population, it could be a much, much higher incidence than currently is being accounted for. Because NLD is not currently defined correctly, it also is not being tracked correctly, and therefore neither are ADD and Autism Spectrum Disorders currently defined or tracked correctly.

If this were the case, NLD not only could stand on its own as an entity in the DSM, but if a lot of the diagnoses of ADD and Asperger's were syphoned off to the NLD spectrum camp, we would have a much clearer idea of how many people with NLD there actually are. Until such a classification occurs, there is no clear and definitive way to know the true incidence and prevalence. But until NLD gets into the DSM, there is no evidence that it's real—which is why it's up to us, all of us, to change that. To find out more about how you can become an NLD advocate and activist, please visit my website.[119]

> You have encouraged me to not give up and do what it takes to be a real success in life. I totally agree that we need to spread the word around about NLD.

Conclusion: what I learned from talking to others with NLD

> Mostly, if I could say one thing to others with NLD, it would be to comfort them, to show them that someone has gone before and things have turned out OK.

In the 12 years I spent working on this project, from doing the research for the psychology paper that led to my thesis that turned into this book, the hundreds of emails from readers I've received and answered, and finally this third edition, I found that many of our previous assumptions about NLD were wrong. Difficulty with math seems to be peripheral, there is no "right-hemisphere disorder," not all executive functioning skills are created equal, and the majority of symptoms do tend to improve, to name just a few.

But more importantly, I've found that we can learn a lot by actually *listening* to what people with NLD have to say about their own experiences, thoughts, and feelings. Undiagnosed or misdiagnosed NLD can lead to an enormous waste of human potential. Earlier diagnosis, earlier intervention, and better preparation on the part of parents, therapists, doctors, and schools are needed. Schools need more funding and more teacher training; parents and therapists need more education. Above all else, more tolerance is needed by all concerned, so that those of us with NLD can achieve our full academic, social, occupational, and spiritual potential.

End Notes

Introduction

1   www.nldfromtheinsideout.com

2   www.booklocker.com

Chapter 1

3   Cobb. J. (2003) *Learning How to Learn: Getting Into and Surviving College When You Have a Learning Disability.* Washington, DC: Child and Family Press, p.7.

4   Katz, L. J., Goldstein, G. and Beers, S. R. (2001) *Learning Disabilities in Older Adolescents and Adults: Clinical Utility of the Neuropsychological Perspective.* New York, Boston, Dordrecht, London, Moscow: Klawer Academic/Plenum Publishers, p.72.

Chapter 2

5   Johnson, D. and Mykelbust, H. (1967) *Learning Disabilities: Educational Principles and Practices.* New York: Grune and Stratton, p.272.

6   *Ibid,* p.273.

7   *Ibid,* p.8.

8   Rourke, B. P. (1989) *Nonverbal Learning Disabilities: The Syndrome and the Model.* New York, London: Guilford Press.

9   Wilderdom (2004) *Wechsler Adult Intelligence Scale (WAIS).* Blaine,WA: Wilderdom. Available at www.wilderdom.com/personality/intelligenceWAISWISC.html, accessed on 1 February 2016.

10   Rourke (1989) *op. cit.* Rourke's theory remains essentially the same in his subsequent books: Rourke, B. P. and Fuerst, D. R. (1991) *Learning Disabilities and Psychosocial Functioning: A Neuropsychological Perspective.* New York, London: The Guilford Press; Rourke, B. P. (1995) *Syndrome of Nonverbal Learning Disabilities: Neurodevelopmental Manifestations.* New York, London: The Guilford Press.

11   Rourke (1989) *op. cit.*

12   See books: Tanguay, P. B. (2001) *Nonverbal Learning Disabilities at Home: A Parent's Guide.* London, Philadelphia: Jessica Kingsley Publishers; Tanguay, P. B. (2002) *Nonverbal Learning Disabilities at School: Educating Students with NLD, Asperger Syndrome, and Related Conditions.* London, Philadelphia: Jessica Kingsley Publishers.

13   In addition to: Thompson, S. (1997) *The Source for Nonverbal Learning Disorders.* East Moline, IL: LinguiSystems.

14   See Stewart, K. (2002) *Helping a Child with Nonverbal Learning Disorder or Asperger's Syndrome.* Oakland, CA: New Harbinger Publications.

15   Palombo, J. (2006) *Nonverbal Learning Disabilities: A Clinical Perspective.* New York, London: W. W. Norton and Company.

16   *Ibid.* pp.125–143.

17   Rourke (1989) *op. cit.* pp.133–5.

18   Cortiella C. and Horowitz. S. H. (2014) *The State of Learning Disabilities: Facts, Trends and Emerging Issues.* New York: National Center for Learning Disabilities. National Center for Learning Disabilities. *The State of Learning Disabilities:* Third Edition, 2014. Available at: www.ncld.org/wp-content/uploads/2014/11/2014-State-of-LD.pdf p.12, accessed on 12 April 2016.

19   www.thelighthouseproject.com

20   Whitney, R. V. (2002) *Bridging the Gap: Raising a Child with Nonverbal Learning Disorder.* New York: Perigee Trade/Penguin Group, p.x (Introduction).

Chapter 3

21   Thompson, S. (1997) *The Source for Nonverbal Learning Disorders.* East Moline, IL: LinguiSystems, pp.167–8.

22   Dobbs, D. (2007) 'The gregarious brain.' *The New York Times,* 8 July, 2007, p.44.

23   Gardner, H. (2000) *Intelligence Reframed: Multiple Intelligences for the 21st Century.* New York: Basic Books.

24   Wechsler, D. (1997) *Wechsler Adult Intelligence Scale®: Third Edition* (WAIS-III). San Antonio, TX: Psychological Corporation. See: www.pearsonclinical.com/psychology/products/100000243/wechsler-adult-intelligence-scale--third-edition-wais-iii.html, accessed on 1 February 2016.

25   Dumont, R. and Willis, J. O. (2002) 'Wechsler Intelligence Scale for Children, 3rd. ed. (WISC-III) 1991.' Teaneck, NJ: Fairleigh Dickinson University. Available at http://alpha.fdu.edu/psychology/WISC-III%20Descrpition_.htm, accessed on 1 February 2016.

26   Rourke (1989) *op. cit.*

27   Tanguay, P. B. (1999) 'NLD = VIQ > PIQ… It ain't necessarily so.' *NLD On The Web!* Available at www.nldontheweb.org/tanguay.htm, accessed on 13 November 2015.

28   Dumont and Willis, *op. cit.*

29   Kaufman, A. S. (1994) *Intelligent Testing with the WISC®-III.* Wiley Series on Personality Processes. New York, Chichester, Brisbane, Toronto, Singapore: John Wiley and Sons, p.150.

30   Wechsler, D. (2008) *Wechsler Adult Intelligence Scale®: Fourth Edition (WAIS-IV).* San Antonio, TX: Psychological Corporation. See: www.pearsonclinical.com/psychology/products/100000392/wechsler-adult-intelligence-scalefourth-edition-wais-iv.html, accessed on 1 February 2016.

31   Wechsler, D. (2014) *Wechsler Intelligence Scale for Children®: Fifth Edition* (WISC-V). San Antonio, TX: Psychological Corporation. See: http://wiscv.com/assets/wisc-v-ebrochure/index.html#1, accessed on 1 February 2016.

32   Tanguay, P. (2002) *Nonverbal Learning Disabilities at School: Educating Students with NLD, Asperger's Syndrome and Related Conditions.* London, Philadelphia: Jessica Kingsley Publishers.

Chapter 4

33   Mader, S. S. (2004) *Biology.* Boston, MA: McGraw-Hill Higher Education.

34   Adapted from: Carter, R. (1998) *Mapping The Mind.* Berkeley, Los Angeles, London: University of California Press, pp.14–7.

35   Doidge, N. (2007) *The Brain That Changes Itself: Stories of Personal Triumph from the Frontiers of Brain Science.* New York: Viking, p.80.

36   Mader, *op. cit.* p.701.

37   *Ibid.*

38   Rourke (1989) *op. cit.*

39   Rourke (1989) *op. cit.*

40   Professor David Stevens. Personal conversation, January, 2006.

Chapter 5

41   Doidge, *op. cit.* p.81.

42   *Ibid.* p.82.

43   Medina, J. (2009) *Brain Rules: 12 Principles for Surviving and Thriving at Work, Home and School.* Seattle: Pear Press, p.174.

44   *Ibid.* p.176.

45   *Ibid.* pp.178–9.

46   Reynolds, G. (2010) 'Phys ed: Can exercise moderate anger?' *The New York Times,* August 11, 2010.

47   Parker-Pope, T. (2010) 'Vigorous exercise linked with better grades.' *The New York Times,* June 3, 2010.

48   Medina, *op. cit.* pp.21–2.

49   Carter, *op. cit.* p.37, p.115, p.129.

50   Gudrais, E. (2010) 'The power of touch.' *Harvard Magazine,* November–December 2010. Available at: http://harvardmagazine.com/2010/11/the-power-of-touch, accessed on 1 February 2016.

Chapter 6

51   Jaffee, E. (2007) 'Mirror neurons: How we reflect on behavior.' *Observer 20,* 5.

52   Doidge, *op. cit.* p.226.

53   Brizendine, L. (2010) *The Male Brain: A Breakthrough Understanding of How Men and Boys Think.* New York: Broadway Books, p.xvi.

54   Hickok, G. (2014) *The Myth of Mirror Neurons: The Real Neuroscience of Communication and Cognition.* New York, London: W. W. Norton and Company.

55   Dutton, K. (2012) *The Wisdom of Psychopaths: What Saints, Spies, and Serial Killers can Teach Us About Success.* New York: Scientific American/Farrar, Strauss, and Giroux, p.17.

56   Brizendine, *op. cit.* p.101.

57   *Ibid.* p.xv.

58   *Ibid.* p.xvi. (Introduction)

59   *Ibid.* p.xvi. (Introduction)

Chapter 7

60   Carter, *op. cit.* p.182.

61   Berk, L. E. (2005) *Infants, Children, and Adolescents.* Boston, MA: Pearson/Allyn and Bacon, pp.220–1.

62   Lehrer, J. (2009) *How We Decide.* New York: Houghton Mifflin.

63   Carter, *op. cit.* p.61, p.182.

Chapter 8

64   Hough, L. (2011) 'You need /r/ /ee/ /d/ to read.' *Harvard Ed. Magazine,* Winter 2011. Available at: www.gse.harvard.edu/news/ed/11/01/you-need-r-ee-d-read, accessed on 2 February 2016.

65   Trafton, A. (2013) 'Brain scans may help diagnose dyslexia.' *McGovern Institute for Brain Research at MIT Newsroom.* Available at: http://mcgovern.mit.edu/news/news/brain-scans-may-help-diagnose-dyslexia/, accessed on 2 February 2016.

66   Doidge, *op. cit.* p.38.

67   Blaszczak-Boxe, A. (2015) 'The brain that just doesn't get numbers.' *Brain Decoder.* Available at: www.braindecoder.com/the-hard-math-problem-of-the-brain-that-no-one-talks-about-1101920476.html, accessed on 2 February 2016.

68   Flora, C. (2013) 'How can a smart kid be so bad at math?' *Discover Magazine,* July/August 2013. Available at: http://discovermagazine.com/2013/julyaug/20-learning-disability-dyscalculia-explains-how-a-smart-kid-can-be-so-bad-at-math, accessed on 2 February 2016.

69   Kaku, M. (2014) *The Future of the Mind: The Scientific Quest to Understand, Enhance, and Empower the Mind.* New York: Anchor.

Chapter 9

70   Seligman, M. (1998) *Learned Optimism: How to Change Your Mind and Your Life.* New York: Free Press/Simon and Schuster, p.15.

71   Peterson, C., Maier, S. F. and Seligman, M.E.P. (1993) *Learned Helplessness: A Theory for the Age of Personal Control.* New York, Oxford: Oxford University Press.

72   Dubin, D. (2009) *Asperger Syndrome and Anxiety: A Guide to Successful Stress Management.* London, Philadelphia: Jessica Kingsley Publishers.

Chapter 12

73   Canty Graves, J. and Graves, C. (2014)
      *Parents Have the Power to Make Special
      Education Work: An Insider Guide.* London:
      Jessica Kingsley Publishers.

74   www.makespecialeducationwork.com

75   The description of the JEAP is here: www.
      bje.org/?specialedu.jeap, and the form is
      here: www.bje.org/downloads/?id=0ee-
      a0793bb168392de955f67d288d2a4.

76   Mooney, J. and Cole, D. (2000) *Learning
      Outside the Lines: Two Ivy League Students with
      Learning Disabilities and ADHD Give You The
      Tools.* New York: Fireside.

77   http://gailshapiro.com/index.php

78   Morgenstern, J. (2004) *Time Management
      from the Inside Out: The Foolproof System
      for Taking Control of Your Schedule – and
      Your Life.* Second edition. New York: Holt
      Paperbacks.

79   Morgenstern, J. (2004) *Organizing from
      the Inside Out, Second Edition: The Foolproof
      System For Organizing Your Home, Your Office
      and Your Life.* Second edition. New York:
      Holt Paperbacks.

80   Walsh, P. (2004) *How to Organize (Just
      About) Everything: More Than 500 Step-
      by-Step Instructions for Everything from
      Organizing Your Closets to Planning a Wedding
      to Creating a Flawless Filing System.* New
      York: Free Press.

81   www.napo.net

82   www.nldfromtheinsideout.com

Chapter 13

83   Black, C. (2011) 'Introverts are taking
      over the world.' *Introvert Zone.* Available
      at: http://introvertzone.com/ratio-of-
      introverts, accessed on 2 February 2016.

84   Editors of Esquire Magazine (2009)
      *Esquire: The Handbook of Style: A Man's
      Guide to Looking Good.* New York: Hearst
      Publishers.

85   Post Senning, C., Post, P. and Watts,
      S. (2007) *Teen Manners: From Malls to
      Meals to Messaging and Beyond.* New York:
      HarperTeen.

86   http://emilypost.com/lifestyle/childrens-
      seminars

87   www.rudebusters.com

88   Nowicki, S. Jr. and Duke, M. P. (2003)
      *Will I Ever Fit In?: The Breakthrough Program
      for Conquering Adult Dyssemia.* Atlanta:
      Peachtree Publishers.

89   www.datingadvice.com/for-men/10-best-
      disabled-dating-sites

90   Madaras, L. and Madaras, A. (2007) *The
      'What's Happening to My Body?' Book for
      Boys.* Revised third edition. New York:
      Newmarket Press.

91   Madaras, L. and Madaras, A. (2007) *The
      'What's Happening to My Body?' Book for
      Girls.* Revised third edition. New York:
      Newmarket Press.

92   Bell Alexander, R. (1998) *Changing Bodies,
      Changing Lives: A Book for Teens on Sex and
      Relationships.* Expanded third edition. New
      York: Random House.

93   Boston Women's Health Book Collective
      (2005) *Our Bodies, Ourselves: A New Edition
      for a New Era.* New York: Touchstone.

94   Koegel, L. and LaZebnik, C. (2009)
      *Growing Up on the Spectrum: A Guide to
      Life, Love, and Learning for Teens and Young
      Adults with Autism and Asperger's.* New York:
      Viking.

Chapter 14

95   Parton, A. and Johnston, L. (2003) *Leaving
      Home: Survival of the Hippest.* Kansas City,
      MO: Andrews McMeel Publishing.

96   Berger, L., Colton, M., Mistry, M., Rossi,
      P., Mandell, Z. and Mandell, J. (2015) *Up
      Your Score: SAT: The Underground Guide,
      2016–2017 Edition.* New York: Workman
      Publishing Company.

97   www.ets.org

98   Cobb, *op. cit.*

99   Simpson, C. and Spencer. V. G. (2009)
      *College Success for Students With Learning
      Disabilities: Strategies and Tips to Make the
      Most of Your College Experience.* Austin:
      Prufrock Press.

100 Berger, L. and Harris, L. (1992) *Tray Gourmet: Be Your Own Chef in the College Cafeteria.* New York: Lake Isle Press.

101 Fast, Y. (2006) *Employment for Individuals With Nonverbal Learning Disabilities and Asperger's Syndrome: Stories and Strategies.* London, Philadelphia: Jessica Kingsley Publishers.

102 Feldblum, C. R., Barry, K. and Benfer, E. A. (2008) 'The ADA Amendments Act of 2008.' *Texas Journal on Civil Liberties and Civil Rights*, Spring, 203.

103 National Council on Disability (2002) *Righting the ADA, No. 1: Introductory Paper.* The Americans With Disabilities Act Policy Brief Series. Washington, DC: National Council on Disability.

104 Feldblum, Barry, Benfer, *op. cit.* p.202.

105 *Ibid.* p.203.

106 *Ibid.* p.204.

107 *Ibid.* p.238.

108 www.eeoc.gov

109 https://adata.org/ada-timeline provides a simple timeline. This link: www.law.georgetown.edu/archiveada/ gives a much more in-depth discussion of the evolution.

110 You can search for an Elder Law attorney in your community at the website of the National Academy of Elder Law Attorneys, Inc., a non-profit organization: www.naela.org.

117 U.S. Department of Health and Human Services Centers for Disease Control and Prevention, Autism Information Center: www.cdc.gov/ncbddd/autism.

118 Alexander, G. (2010) Personal interview, 18 August 2010.

119 www.nldfromtheinsideout.com

Chapter 16

111 Strohl, M. P. (2011) 'Bradley's benzedrine studies on children with behavioral disorders.' *Yale Journal of Biology and Medicine 84*, 1, 27–33.

112 *Ibid.*

113 Silberman, S. (2015) *Neurotribes: The Legacy of Autism and the Future of Neurodiversity.* New York: Avery.

114 *Ibid.* pp.180–3.

115 *Ibid.* pp.98–9.

116 *Ibid.* p.168.

Index